IF THE DEVIL "MADE" YOU DO IT,

YOU BLEW IT!

(But It Doesn't Need To Happen Again)

IF THE DEVIL "MADE" YOU DO IT,

YOU BLEW IT!

(But It Doesn't Need To Happen Again)

LORRAINE PETERSON

BETHANY HOUSE PUBLISHERS

MINNEAPOLIS, MINNESOTA 55438

A Division of Bethany Fellowship, Inc.

Published by Bethany House Publishers
A Division of Bethany Fellowship, Inc.
6820 Auto Club Road, Minneapolis, Minnesota 55438

Printed in the United States of America

Library of Congress Cataloging-in-Publication Data

Peterson, Lorraine.
    If the devil made you do it, you blew it! / Lorraine Peterson.
        p.   cm. — (Devotionals for teens)
        Summary: Advises teenagers on overcoming temptation, whether it be overeating on cookies, cheating on a test, or killing a policeman.

        1. Teenagers—Prayer-books and devotions—English.
2. Temptation—Meditations. [1. Temptation.] I. Title. II. Series.
BT725.P37   1989
248.8'3—dc20   89-36221
ISBN 1-55661-052-1   CIP

I'd like to dedicate this book
to all the teenagers I've worked
with both in the United States
and Mexico.

About the Author

LORRAINE PETERSON was born in Red Wing, Minnesota, grew up on a farm near Ellsworth, Wisconsin, and now resides in Guadalajara, Mexico. She received her B.A. (in history) from North Park College in Chicago, and has taken summer courses from the University of Minnesota and the University of Mexico in Mexico City.

Lorraine has taught high school and junior high. She has been an advisor to interdenominational Christian clubs in Minneapolis public schools and has taught teenage Bible studies. She has written seven bestselling devotional books for teens:

If God Loves Me, Why Can't I Get My Locker Open?
Falling Off Cloud Nine and Other High Places
Why Isn't God Giving Cash Prizes?
Real Characters in the Making
Dying of Embarrassment & Living to Tell About It
Anybody Can Be Cool, But Awesome Takes Practice
If the Devil Made You Do It, You Blew It!

Acknowledgements

I appreciate the insights given me by the authors whose books I read as background material for writing this manuscript: *Temptation* by Dietrich Bonhoffer; *The Purpose of Temptation* by Bob Mumford; *My Body, His Life* by Paul G. Trulin; *Temptation* by John C. Souter; *Temptation: Help for Struggling Christians* by Charles Durham; *Trial of Your Faith* and *Overcoming Temptation* by Hugh Smith; and *Temptation* by Charles Stanley.

I'd also like to give credit to Dr. Bill and Anabel Gilham and Dr. Bruce Thompson whose taped messages have formed the basis of some of these devotionals.

Finally, I'd like to thank family and friends for helping and supporting me during the writing of this book. My father went a lot further than the extra mile to locate an out-of-print book I wanted, and helped in many other ways. My Aunt Lois double-checked some facts I couldn't research in Guadalajara. My nieces and nephews—Beth, Brett, Karri, and Kirk—sent encouraging "fan mail." My roommate, Juanita, has faithfully prayed for me and this book. Finally, I want to express my gratitude to Michael O'Connor for proofreading my manuscript and giving many excellent suggestions.

Other Teen Devotionals
from Bethany House Publishers

Contents

10

A *Personal Word*

Whenever young people at retreats and youth conferences anonymously write out questions they'd like answered, I've found that roughly half of these queries deal with the subject of temptation. This is as true of inner-city kids as suburban kids who attend private schools; it makes no difference if you ask junior highs or senior highs; it's the same in Mexico as in the United States. Tom Harringer, who has worked on Campus Crusade's youth staff for 22 years and who was my director when I served as a volunteer leader, makes this statement:

> Young people often ask me, "How can I overcome temptation?" Some students find it difficult to identify temptation when it comes, because in today's culture many people call good "evil" and evil "good" without really knowing the difference.
>
> Young people need help to determine the differences between right and wrong, and to *choose* to follow God's direction in the power of the Holy Spirit. I find that teenagers have a great interest in discovering that they have the *power* to *do* the right thing.

Surprisingly, little has been written about temptation even though temptation is part of daily life. Because the way it is handled makes the difference between victory and defeat, I wanted to write something on this theme for teenagers. This book goes beyond the "if-in-doubt-*don't*" format. It also explores the purpose of temptation and the root problems that make us vulnerable to Satan's "suggestions." The main emphasis is placed not on the decadence of these last days but on our all-powerful Christ. It is my prayer that it will provide practical encouragement for many young people.

How to Use This Book

Memorizing, digesting, meditating, and obeying Scripture is the proven way of resisting temptation. It's the only method Jesus used. Because it is a key to victory in your Christian life, I'd suggest that after reading each devotional, you copy the verse on a card to carry around with you all day—even though this book gives you a lot of other assignments to provide variety. During each natural break, spend time hiding that verse in your heart, reading it through and emphasizing a different word each time, putting your name and your circumstances into the verse, and deciding how you must change your life so you can fully obey the verse.

You'll be surprised how many opportunities there are each day to meditate on Scripture:

while combing or drying your hair
waiting for a friend
during class free time
when snacking, or eating alone
during TV commercials
sunbathing
waiting in line
marking time before the end-of-the-hour bell rings
when jogging or walking
while spending time with a good friend (quiz each other
    on the memory work and compare notes on what the
    verse means in your life.)
and most important, while falling asleep each night.

If you use this book to help form a lifelong practice of Scripture meditation, your spiritual growth will be marked. Make it a habit to pick out verses that directly speak to the problem you're experiencing. If your arsenal is full of verses to hurl at the Devil, then no matter what the temptation, you will experience more and more victory in your life!

Part One

The Rules of the Game

CHAPTER 1

If The Devil "Made" You Do It, You Blew It!

Jay sat in the back seat of the squad car, oblivious to the pouring rain that blurred the neon sign and city lights. Beyond the foggy glass, they became only swirls of brightness and color, contrasting sharply with the inky blackness of the night. During the ten-minute ride to the police station, his mind reviewed the events that had preceded his arrest.

Jay had rebelled against his strict parents and had started running around with the fast-lane crowd. He stopped going to church, his grades went down, and he had frequent fights with his parents. Drinking, drugs, and danger had seemed like a lot of "fun."

His new friends loved adventure and excitement as much as he did. Hang gliding, motorcycle racing and mountain climbing challenged them for a while—but boredom always seemed to catch up with the boys. The party at Dave's house that evening turned out to be a real bummer. Dave had pulled out two pistols and suggested they do something really crazy—like rob the MacDonalds on the corner. He said he'd seen the perfect plot on a TV show, and they organized for action. Though Jay had experienced a twinge of conscience, he agreed to go along with the gang and drive the getaway car. The only problem was that a police cruiser was only a half-block away. When it wheeled into the lot, everybody ran. And everybody got away—except Jay.

When they arrived at the station, he knew the police

had all the evidence they needed. In the excitement of planning their strategy, Jay had forgotten to take his bill-fold out of his pocket. His car was still sitting back in the MacDonalds' lot, where the cruiser had blocked him in, barring his escape. Realizing there was no way out, Jay answered all the questions truthfully.

Hours later, at 4:00 A.M., his parents arrived at the station. His mom was crying and his dad looked pale and nervous. "Son, why did you participate in a holdup?" his mother agonized. "How could you do such a thing?"

Jay paused for a moment and then muttered, "The Devil made me do it."

And he was serious.

When we hear something often enough—even if it's a lie—we tend to believe it. Brainwashing, political prop-aganda, and advertising are built on this fact. A cliche that's tossed around a lot is the one Jay fell for: "The Devil made me do it." The little boy who eats all the chocolate chip cookies, the junior high girl who cheats on the final, and the young man who kills a policeman have one thing in common: all feel as if they are dealing with some irre-sistible, evil force. And somehow, "The Devil made me do it" seems like an adequate explanation of what took place. But is it really true? The Bible teaches that God has given human beings the ability to choose between right and wrong and that He holds us totally responsible for our actions. "Choose for yourselves this day whom you will serve. . . . But as for me and my household, we will serve the Lord" (Josh. 24:15). "The soul who sins is the one who will die" (Ezek. 18:20). "Be sure that your sin will find you out" (Num. 32:23).

We are not puppets or robots. Because God created us with free wills, He will not force us to obey Him. Nor is the Devil able to control us unless we somehow permit him to do so. But the Devil *is* the world's most clever con man, and he constantly tries to trick you and me into thinking that our only choice is to sin. But that is never true. Even in a wouldn't-you-steal-food-to-save-the-life-of-your-starving-child kind of situation, the person who believes in a God who answers prayer and performs miracles has an alternative to breaking God's commandments.

"Resist the Devil, and he *will* flee from you" (James 4:7, emphasis *added*) is still in the Bible and it's *still* true! So if you say, "The Devil made me do it"—*you* blew it.

MEMORIZE

"I saw Satan fall like lightning from heaven. [Because he no longer has any real power.] I have given you authority to trample on snakes and scorpions, and to overcome all the power of the enemy" (Luke 10:18–19).

PICTURE THIS

PERSONALIZE AND READ OUT LOUD

When Satan pulls his power play, I'll remember that Jesus saw him fall like lightning from heaven. When evil seems irresistible, I'll remember that Jesus gave me authority over that sneaky snake, the Devil. In Jesus' name I can rise above every obstacle the evil one puts in my way.

PRAY THE VERSE, APPLYING IT TO YOUR LIFE

Dear God, thank you that Satan fell from heaven and that Jesus defeated him on the cross. Thank you that I'll be victorious over _____ and _____ (present temptations in your life). With Jesus-Power I'll be an overcomer.

STOMPING ON SOME "SNAKES AND SCORPIONS"

List the biggest problems and temptations you face. Claim your authority as a Christian to trample on the Devil, the force behind these problems. Remember that the *only* tactic available to Satan is to wear you out so *you* surrender to him. Hold on to the victory that is yours!

CHAPTER 2

A Pain With a Purpose

Ryan, an avid science fiction fan, was reading a story with a rather weird plot.

A mad scientist bent on revenge succeeded in producing a race of people who experienced no pain. No one ever suffered from headaches, muscle strain, or stomach discomfort. Children often died from burns because they had no nerve signals to keep them away from fires. It was common for people to drop dead while laughing, conversing, or resting, and no one had any inkling why they had died. A little child once exclaimed in excitement, "Look, the bus hit me and now I have red streaks all over!" The sadistic scientist got his satisfaction from seeing the society suffer.

Reading the book made Ryan remember his emergency appendectomy. He'd gone to school one morning feeling just fine. But after lunch he experienced a pain in his abdomen that doubled him over. He'd been rushed to the hospital emergency room where doctors operated just in time. If his appendix had burst he might have died.

Ryan had never thought of pain as a friend, but after his appendectomy he could see its usefulness.

Have you ever asked the question, "Why doesn't God just strike the Devil dead?" He could, you know. It might seem strange to you that a good and all-powerful God would permit the Devil to keep deceiving, tormenting, and badgering people.

But even Satan must serve God's purposes. Physical

pain—hideous, annoying and, at times, nearly unbearable—indicates that something is wrong with your body and tells you it's time to see a doctor. In the same way, Satan's temptations uncover sinful heart attitudes. Once we sense we're being tempted, you and I can draw closer to Jesus where we can receive the help we need.

It works like this. As the Devil tries to make you commit sin, he uncovers thought patterns that are the root of your wrongdoing. For instance, he spotlights the jealousy deep down inside when he tries to make you lash out at someone you resent. Then you know it's time to make an appointment with Dr. Jesus, the Great Physician, and let His supernatural surgery remove that jealousy from your spirit.

Whenever the Devil's temptation brings ugly things to the surface, let the Holy Spirit show you if the problem is your sin, false guilt, or a need for inner healing. "When he [the Counselor, the Holy Spirit] comes, he will convict the world of guilt in regard to sin and righteousness and judgment" (John 16:8).

The Devil's activity should always drive you straight into the arms of Jesus: confessing sin and receiving forgiveness so you can go on in victory, obtaining the assurance that "there is now no condemnation for those who are in Christ Jesus," and letting Him heal the emotional wounds you've suffered.

The Devil is a pain with a purpose. God can use Satan's evil designs for your good. The Devil's turbulence can drive you ever closer to Jesus, the sin eradicator, and the source of joy, peace, and comfort.

MEMORIZE

"In this you greatly rejoice, though now for a little while you may have had to suffer grief in all kinds of trials. These have come so that your faith—of greater worth than gold, which perishes even though refined by fire—may be proved genuine and may result in praise, glory and honor when Jesus Christ is revealed" (1 Pet. 1:6–7).

PICTURE THIS

PERSONALIZE AND READ OUT LOUD

I will find my joy in the hope Jesus offers even though I'm suffering through trials, like _____ and _____ . I know these have come to show me whether or not my faith is the real thing. My genuine faith—minus all the fakeness—will bring praise and glory to Jesus.

PRAY THE VERSE, APPLYING IT TO YOUR LIFE

Dear God, help me to rejoice in the middle of trouble, keeping my eyes on the hope I have in you. Thank you that these trials will expose hypocrisy and sin so I can get rid of the garbage in my life and have a faith that will truly honor you.

MEDITATE ON SCRIPTURE

Write 1 Pet. 1:6–7 on a card and take it with you today. When your mind is free, concentrate on the words of this verse and let them become part of you. Fall asleep repeating the words of this verse.

CHAPTER 3

Don't Let the Devil's Masquerade Fool You

Alexis couldn't understand it. She had memorized 2 Cor. 5:17: "Therefore, if anyone is in Christ, he is a new creation; the old has gone, the new has come!" If the old life was really gone, as the verse said, why did she think so often of going back to her old group of friends? Why did looking through her closet make her wish she could go shoplifting with her girlfriend just once more?

When she attended the weekly Bible study on Thursday night, their teacher, Marilyn, affirmed, "The *old* you that enjoys sinning is dead. The *sinful* you died with Jesus on the cross, so you're not addicted to doing wrong anymore. If you don't believe it, just look up Romans 6:6: 'For we know that our old self was crucified with him so that the body of sin might be rendered powerless, that we should no longer be slaves to sin.' "

And at that very moment, Alexis was thinking that getting high would be the best way to escape her problems.

Alexis decided to talk to Marilyn after class. "Everything you said about not being addicted to sin anymore—and that verse I learned about being a new creation—well, they sound real cool. But I keep thinking about going shoplifting and getting high and wearing something really sexy so all the guys will notice me. When I dress like a 'Christian,' nobody ever asks me out."

Marilyn smiled. "Alexis, you have to learn the rules of the game. And the Devil never plays fair.

"First of all, your brain is really a chunk of meat that houses a fantastic computer. It forms thought patterns based on past experiences and on things you've read, heard, and seen. The Devil, who is the world's cleverest con man, uses these 'computer printouts' not only to put thoughts into your mind but to impersonate you. He'll pose as Alexis with a feminine Texas accent and speak into your mind, 'I really need a hit.' Or he'll feed you this line: 'I can't stand not having boys whistle at me, and I know just what I need to wear to attract their attention.' Once he convinces you that *you* thought all that, he can go on to the next step—his ultimate weapon. 'The Bible must not be true,' he whispers. 'It says the old has gone, but I can see that real life is different.'

"Romans 7:20–22 tells us how this all works out in the life of a defeated Christian. 'Now if I do what I do not want to do, it is no longer I who do it [because I really am a new creature in Christ], but it is sin living in me that does it [these old patterns in my brain, which is programmed to bring up desires of my former life]. So I find this law at work: When I want to do good, evil is right there with me [the Devil masquerading as me]. For in my inner being [the new me that has eternal life], I delight in God's law.'

"In other words," said Marilyn, "the *new* you loves to obey God. That's why you now feel guilty for things that never used to bother you. However, the Devil's masquerade is so clever that instead of unmasking him, you just assume that the *real* you wants drugs or stolen clothes, or constant attention from boys.

"The truth is that God has made you over again into a transformed person. You need to accept that as fact and begin acting as the new Alexis you really are. When the Devil comes disguised as you, reject each thought he gives you—and remember that you have no guilt—unless you buy the Devil's idea and run with it."

Don't let the Devil's masquerade fool you. Next time he attacks, just say, "Mr. Devil, I'm not listening to your suggestion. Beat it, in the name of Jesus!"

MEMORIZE

"Satan himself masquerades as an angel of light. It is not surprising, then, if his servants masquerade as servants of righteousness" (2 Cor. 11:14–15).

PICTURE THIS

PERSONALIZE AND READ OUT LOUD

If the Devil runs around posing as an angel, he certainly could impersonate me! He also has a lot of false teachers and fakes masquerading as servants of God.

PRAY THE VERSE, APPLYING IT TO YOUR LIFE

Dear God, help me to stay so close to you and to know your Word so well that I'll recognize the Devil, even when he's playing the part of someone else—even me.

GARBAGE ELIMINATION PROJECT

List the things the Devil tries to convince you to do as he uses the results of wrongly ingrained patterns. For example: "I can't live without Dave, my non-Christian boyfriend. I hate my father for what he did to me." Over each of these, write out 2 Cor. 5:17 in red ink. Decide not to accept these Devilish ideas.

CHAPTER 4

The Teacher Called Temptation

Robbie and Jason had been best friends since third grade and were always together. The kids at church and school often referred to them as Frick and Frack. Jason was a straight-A student, and Robbie usually got B's and C's. On the other hand, Robbie was a top player on the football team, while Jason warmed the bench. But because they were such good friends, neither one felt any jealousy toward the other.

But when Robbie was voted captain of the football team (which was favored to win the city championship), he became a local celebrity. His picture was in the paper, he appeared on the *Sports Tonight* show, good-looking girls tried to get his attention, and he enjoyed instant popularity at school. He started dating Cherry, the beautiful blonde homecoming queen, and began to hang around with the "in crowd."

One day before English class, Jason reminded him of plans they had made to go duck hunting. Robbie brushed him aside. "Tonight I have a date with Cherry, and tomorrow I have a TV interview. Ducks just aren't on my agenda anymore."

As Jason walked away, Robbie noticed the terribly hurt look on his face. Suddenly, he realized what was happening. Popularity had gone to his head. He knew that Cherry wasn't a Christian, so he had no business dating her—even if she was the prettiest girl in the whole school. And after he began hanging out with the "in crowd," he'd started drinking just

27

a little so he wouldn't feel out of place.

Now, the expression he had seen on Jason's face cut through him. Jason was the most faithful friend and the best Christian he had ever known! How could he dump him just because he didn't fit into his popularity trip? Robbie had always prided himself on not being a fake. How could he have fallen into this trap?

Can you identify with Robbie? Have you ever thought, "That will never happen to me"—only to find yourself doing the very thing you hate? What's the next step?

Someone has said, "There's nothing like temptation to show what you'll do if given the chance." Bob Mumford, in his book *The Purpose of Temptation*, says the Greek word that we translate as "temptation" in the Bible, actually means "that which puts us to the proof—whether by good or malicious design."* God allows temptation to exist in this world because it brings out what is really inside our hearts.

Robbie didn't know that he'd compromise his Christian testimony and drop his best friend for the sake of popularity—until the opportunity presented itself. Now that this hidden defect is out in the open, he must confess the sin of caring more about what the other kids think than about what God thinks. He must ask God's forgiveness, make the necessary changes in his life, and then go on in victory.

Temptation is part of life, and you can learn to work it to your advantage. Like fire, temptation can destroy you or serve as your assistant. When you get caught off guard and fall for a temptation you thought you were immune to, decide that you'll learn something from the teacher called temptation. Be thankful that you've discovered the slow leak that could someday cause even greater problems. Confess your sin and ask God to root out the pride, or bitterness, or unforgiveness, or whatever caused you to fall. Readjust your life and walk on with Jesus just a little wiser from the lesson temptation taught you.

---

*Bob Mumford. *The Purpose of Temptation*, (Old Tappan, N.J.: Fleming H. Revell Company, 1973), 17.

MEMORIZE

"It was good for me to be afflicted, so that I might learn your decrees" (Ps. 119:71).

PICTURE THIS

PERSONALIZE AND READ OUT LOUD

I know that God allows faith tests in the form of temptations, problems, and difficulties to drive me into His Word so I can learn His truths in deeper ways.

PRAY THE VERSE, APPLYING IT TO YOUR LIFE

Dear God, thank you for the trials and temptations I face. I even thank you for _____ (biggest, present problem). I know that from it I can learn where I'm depending on my own resources and reasoning and not upon you and your Word. Help me to learn more about obeying your commands.

TEMPTATION RESUMÉ

List at least three spiritual lessons you've already learned from facing trials and temptations. Which lessons have you learned the hard way? Also recall the times when you have grown stronger because you resisted temptation at the outset. Decide that you will let temptation be your teacher.

CHAPTER 5

Thou Shalt Not Live by "Big Mac Attacks"

It was the first day of school, and Annie wondered what her new teachers would be like.

She was surprised when her history instructor handed her a long test with impossible questions. She could hardly find one question that she would even *attempt* to answer. But when she looked around and saw all the class "brains" just staring into space, she felt a lot better. It was obvious that nobody could fill in those blanks.

I was that teacher and Annie was my student. Why did I give my pupils a terribly hard test the first day of class? I needed to prove a point—that my students didn't know everything in that boring brown world history book.

You see, the school administration—in their less than infinite wisdom—had changed the social studies program, requiring that I teach the *same* course from the *same* book to the *same* students who had taken it the year before! It's the only test I ever designed to make sure that every student failed (and I promised not to count it if my students agreed never to mention that they had studied the same thing last year).

But it wasn't my *test* that was so bad. It was that nobody was prepared for it. After carefully teaching the material, I could have given the same exam with very different results.

The temptations of life are kind of like standardized tests. The test itself is not good or bad. Your experience with it depends on your preparation and your character.

Everyone sees provocative billboards, has a chance to experiment with drugs, has opportunity to disobey parents and teachers, and is presented with situations where selfishness is the easiest option.

In the drama of temptation there are three characters: you, God, and the Devil. It's kind of like preparing for the standardized test with two teachers.

Mr. Good is interested in your welfare, always speaks the truth and does everything to prepare you for the test. But *Mr. Mean* is cruel and dishonest. He wants everyone to fail, so he gives them wrong information and tries to keep them from studying. Your fate depends on which teacher you follow. And when the exam is administered, Mr. Mean may be the only teacher in sight. He'll whisper wrong answers in your ear and try to keep you from concentrating. But if you succeed in ignoring him and stick to the truth explained by Mr. Good, you'll pass the test and be hardier for having overcome the trial.

God uses even *bad* things to fit into His plan. He permits the Devil to give us hard tests, and His purpose is that we grow wiser because of them. As 1 Cor. 10:13 assures us, "God is faithful; he will not let you be tempted beyond what you can bear."

Believe it or not, you can study for these temptation tests. You can hide God's Word in your heart so that you don't sin. But you must believe and obey that Word by faith. Because when the temptation test is given, you may *feel* as if God is nowhere in sight and that Satan has already decided on your grade. It's not that God has forsaken you; it's just that you don't feel His presence.

God even has a purpose in removing the sense of His presence: It's not unlike the test mother gives little Johnny by asking him not to touch the freshly baked chocolate chip cookies while she's at the grocery store. It's the only way to find out if you're totally faithful to Him! God gave Hezekiah this kind of test. We read in 2 Chron. 32:31, "God left him to test him and to know everything that was in his heart."

God chose to give you a free will, to allow the Devil to

give you temptation tests, and to provide a heavenly handbook with all the answers to the questions. You can give in to one temptation after another. Or you can believe His Word, walk by faith and obey Him.

If you decide to eliminate your the-temptation-was-just-too-strong-for-me mentality and realize that God's Word can bail you out every time, you'll join Jesus as conqueror over temptation. You'll discover that teenagers don't have to live by bread alone—or by illicit sex, or by self-centeredness, or by Big Mac attacks—but by every word that proceeds from the mouth of God.

MEMORIZE

"Blessed is the man who perseveres under trial, because when he has stood the test, he will receive the crown of life that God has promised to those who love him" (James 1:12).

PICTURE THIS

PERSONALIZE AND READ OUT LOUD

I receive a blessing when I stand firm during times of temptation, because after I have passed my temptation test, I will receive the crown of life that God has promised to those who love Him.

PRAY THE VERSE, APPLYING IT TO YOUR LIFE

Dear God, help me to stick with you when trials like _____ (present problem) come. Thank you for the promise that I will receive a crown of life if I love you enough to resist temptation.

MEDITATE ON SCRIPTURE

Copy this verse on a card and carry it around with you all day. Whenever your mind is free, think about this verse and let it change you. Go to sleep thinking about this verse.

CHAPTER 6

Room 314 Survival Skills

Matt Wilson looked forward to the first day of senior high with excitement—and fear. He walked into the immense building, found the lunchroom, lined up with the W's and received his schedule. The first thing he read was, "World History I, Room 314."

After climbing an incredible number of stairs, he puffed his way down the crowded corridor. Once he entered the room, he felt as if he had switched planets. The windowless walls were painted black and there was a fluorescent green rug on the floor. Instead of desks, the room was filled with white sofas and reclining chairs. Rock music proclaimed, *"Alexander was the greatest! Man! He smashed the Assyrian Empire. Alexander was the greatest! Man! He set Rome on fire."*

The teacher, with punk hair and a pin through his ear, assured them that this class was going to be "fun." He passed out psychedelic colored books with great cartoons. The title of chapter 1 caught Matt's eye: "The Roman Emperor Who Secretly Married Queen Victoria." Chapter 2 sounded just as interesting: "The Day Marco Polo Climbed an Egyptian Pyramid." Matt had never been a good student and he had always hated history—but this surely looked more interesting than the courses he had nearly failed before!

In the coming weeks, he listened to the music, soaked in the teacher's crazy lectures and really got into the text. He even studied for the test! However, when he got his paper back, he saw a big red *zero*.

A classmate saw the shocked look on his face and smiled. "You mean you *believed* all that junk? Couldn't you tell this guy was a fake? His purpose was to make all of us fail the history department's standardized tests. I got the regular textbook from the library and studied that. I never listened to a word this guy said, and I got a 95."

At that point, Matt woke up. He was glad it was only a dream—and a very weird one at that!

If you'll look at the world and compare its standard behavior with the commandments in the Word of God, you'll realize that the Devil, just like the teacher in the dream, is relentlessly setting people up to fail. Whether through TV programs, radio announcements, or popular songs, the world is pushing hard for you to accept ideas contrary to the Bible: Illicit sex is okay. If it feels good do it. Do your own thing. Win by intimidation—the list goes on.

Some people have studied so much wrong material that they're bound to fail nearly every temptation test. Worse yet, some sincere Christians get as hoodwinked as Matt. They've digested so many falsehoods they don't even know what truth is, and they don't even realize that their lives are all messed up because of sin.

If you hear wrong information often enough, it's pretty easy to believe it. Hitler knew that, and so he initiated a major propaganda campaign against Jewish people. Communism uses every available opportunity to indoctrinate.

The Devil is no dummy, and his Big Lie campaign will follow you wherever you go. He uses novels, rock music, T-shirt messages, movies, textbooks, advice from friends—every possible method to drum lies into you. If he can get you to believe those lies, you'll fail all the temptation tests.

For instance, if the Devil can make you think that God has been unfair to you, you'll succumb to every attack of depression and self-pity. If you believe that you're superior racially, intellectually, or socially, you'll fall into pride and the sin of putting others down. If you decide that some people are born to be homosexuals, you'll proclaim that homosexual acts aren't sin and that God cannot change desires and lifestyles.

Actually, the world you live in is very much like Room 314. It's full of lies and false information designed by the Devil to destroy you. The only hope we have is to study, to obey, to love, and to memorize the true textbook—the Holy Bible, the only handbook on Room 314 survival skills.

MEMORIZE

"The god of this age [Satan] has blinded the minds of unbelievers, so that they cannot see the light of the gospel of the glory of Christ, who is the image of God" (2 Cor. 4:4).

PICTURE THIS

PERSONALIZE AND READ OUT LOUD

The Devil will always try to blind me from seeing the truth in God's Word. He will attempt to plant unbelief so I don't see the glory of Christ, who is the image of God.

PRAY THE VERSE, APPLYING IT TO YOUR LIFE

Dear God, keep Satan from blinding me to truth and putting unbelief in my heart. Help me see the glory of Christ, because He is the mirror by which I see you.

UNPACKING A PACK OF LIES

List everything you've heard or read in the last month that is based on a false premise. Using scripture, explain why the idea is incorrect.

CHAPTER 7

What's That "Blame Game" Disk Doing in Your Mental Computer?

Glancing at himself hurriedly in the mirror, Tim whipped a comb through his hair. Then he sat down at his desk to read a chapter in his Bible before dashing downstairs for a bite of breakfast and rushing off to school.

Bowing his head, he thanked God for His love, then began to pray for his family and his friends. At that moment, dreadful thoughts entered his head: He should really get back at Mike for stealing his girlfriend. And as the school's office computer assistant, he knew he could get revenge by lowering all Mike's quarter grades.

A minute later, Tim felt utterly ashamed for having such an idea. How could a dedicated Christian like himself devise such a scheme? After all, Mike was also a believer, and Christians were supposed to love one another no matter what. Tim berated himself for being capable of such deceitful thoughts.

The chiming of the clock in the hall told him that he had to go or he'd be late to school. He hadn't even opened his Bible! Completely discouraged, he was sure his day would be awful.

It was.

Have you ever experienced similar difficulties when you sit down to spend some time with God? You need to discover the reason for Tim's problems—and yours. The Devil is perfectly capable of putting thoughts into your head. He might even come up with losers like these: "If you killed your mother, using the strategy you saw on

Murder Mystery, nobody would ever know!" "Just jump off the high bridge, and then the people will feel sorry for treating you so badly." "You're such a lousy Christian you might as well give up right now." The Devil puts the idea in your head and then makes you feel guilty for having thought it!

Hannah Whithall Smith once said that Satan is just like a burglar entering a home, and when the owner tries to chase him out, the intruder turns around and accuses the owner of being the thief! How ridiculous! In order to keep Satan from catching you in this trap, there are some facts you need to know.

First, realize that you are not responsible for the thought the Devil gives you—unless you make it your own. Getting dressed after gym class, you may hear some dirty jokes. If you ignore what is being said and leave as quickly as possible, you've done nothing wrong. However, if you take it all in and add a few of your own, you've fallen into sin. It's the same with the thoughts the Devil sends your way. If you reject them, no matter how foul and terrible, you can go on your way victorious and joyful.

Second, recognize that *every* suggestion of evil comes from the Devil. Satan knows that if he appeared to you in a vision, saying, "I'm the Devil and I've come to make you sin," you'd never buy his goods. So he sneaks up on you, trying to convince you that *you* thought such a horrible thing. Then he can make you feel guilty. Next, he accuses you and leaves you discouraged. Once you lose your confidence, it's a lot easier to get trapped into sinning.

Third, remember that any pride you have in being a "good Christian" will cause you to stumble. Any time you are not totally depending on God, you can be tricked. Don't forget that *all* your righteousness is given to you. It all comes from Jesus.

Don't let the Devil discourage you by putting a bad thought into your head and then accusing you of having come up with such a sinful idea. When the Devil sneaks the "Blame Game" disk into your computer, eject it immediately!

MEMORIZE

"We demolish arguments and every pretension that sets itself up against the knowledge of God. And we take captive every thought to make it obedient to Christ" (2 Cor. 10:5).

PICTURE THIS

PERSONALIZE AND READ OUT LOUD

I won't buy any idea that's contrary to the Bible. I must learn how to catch all the bad thoughts the Devil puts into my head and drive them out. I will consciously set my mind on God's Word and think thoughts that Jesus would approve of.

PRAY THE VERSE, APPLYING IT TO YOUR LIFE

Dear God, help me to discover each thought put into my mind by the Devil and to make my mind obey Jesus. Help me to think on Scripture instead of daydreaming and dwelling on unpleasant episodes in my life.

MEDITATE ON SCRIPTURE

Copy 2 Cor. 10:5 on a card and carry it with you today. Use every spare moment to think about the words of this verse. Let its message penetrate deep into your spirit. Fall asleep with 2 Cor. 10:5 running through your mind.

CHAPTER 8

Listen to the Boss Inside

Tom was good-natured, easygoing—and overweight. His theology was simple: "If God gave me a good appetite, then I should be able to eat whatever I want. After all, God supplied the ingredients and gave men the intelligence to make ice cream and chocolate bars."

If Tom didn't have time to study, he felt that a C− in chemistry was God's will—under the circumstances. If he wanted some extra sleep or felt like doing nothing, why should he fight his "God-given personality"?

When Tom started dating Dana, he fell head-over-heels in love with her. She was so vivacious, so energetic—and so beautiful. Nothing was too good for Dana. He gave her expensive presents and took her to the nicest places. Since God created the physical attraction a guy has for a girl, he considered it his right to enjoy all the kisses and hugs he could sneak in. But he kept craving more and more. Finally he told Dana he loved her so much he wanted to go to bed with her. Dana was shocked. "That would be a *sin*," she insisted.

"But," Tom countered, "God created sex, so it's got to be good. He gave us these desires, so it can't be *that* wrong."

Have you ever heard that line? Have you ever used it yourself? Then there's a fact you need to know. Temptation often involves something good, such as *meeting* a legitimate need. The problem is that *good* desire leads to a bad action if done in the wrong place, or at the wrong time, or with the wrong person. Wrong motives or an appetite out of control also puts normally acceptable behavior in the category of sin.

Turning your portable radio on full blast during the Sunday morning sermon is not only inappropriate, but it will interfere with the reception of God's life-giving Word. The person who eats ten candy bars in one sitting is labeled a glutton. Although sex outside of marriage is sin, it's a beautiful experience when used as God intended. In the garden of Eden, the Devil succeeded in making Adam and Eve believe that something as simple as eating a piece of fruit could never be wrong. He hasn't changed his strategy.

Although many have tried to reduce Christianity to a series of rules and regulations just like other religions, it can't be done. That's why the Holy Spirit lives inside every true Christian to give us the light of His wisdom, to comfort, and to guide. He tells you what loving your neighbor means. He explains the difference between legitimate desires and coveting (wanting something that belongs to someone else). Only the Holy Spirit can tell you the difference between selfish lust and real love.

Watchman Nee, a Chinese Christian who lost his life to the Communists, wrote of a missionary who visited his illiterate new converts. They told the man that when a member of a sect with false teaching had entered their home, they had rejected everything he said.

"How did you know that what the man said, with an open Bible in front of him, was wrong?" questioned the missionary.

"I only listened to the boss inside" was the reply.

In order to overcome temptation, you must listen to the "boss inside," the Holy Spirit. Next double-check that with the compass *outside,* the Holy Scriptures. Then the deceitful Devil will have a hard time fooling you.

MEMORIZE

"The mind of sinful man is death, but the mind controlled by the Spirit is life and peace" (Rom. 8:6).

PICTURE THIS

PERSONALIZE AND READ OUT LOUD

If I follow my own desires and my own reasoning, that will lead to sin and death. But as I obey the Holy Spirit who interprets God's Word and applies it to my circumstances, I'll live.

PRAY THE VERSE, APPLYING IT TO YOUR LIFE

Forgive me, Lord, for trying to make _____ seem okay to do when your Word says it's wrong. I'll distrust my own reasoning and let my mind be controlled by the Holy Spirit so I can enjoy His peace.

MIND CONTROL—THE RIGHT KIND

Carry a copy of Rom. 8:6 with you this month. Every time you feel angry, depressed, or upset repeat the verse and ask the Holy Spirit to control your mind and give you life and peace.

CHAPTER 9

Making Points for God's Team

Shawn felt as if he were involved in a boxing match that never seemed to end. He was probably in round 10,602, but no bell rang to signal a break. The Devil was always finding ways to get at him.

Monday was typical. While he was grabbing a couple of doughnuts and a cup of instant hot chocolate for breakfast, his brother appeared in the doorway, wearing Shawn's new sweater. He exploded. "You're such a lazy leech! If you want nice clothes, earn your own money as I do. Don't you dare touch any of my things without asking me!"

An ugly argument ensued, and afterward Shawn felt guilty for not having more patience with his younger brother. The argument also caused him to be late for school, where the assistant principal's secretary yelled at him for not filling out his tardy pass correctly. His impertinent reply was overheard by Mr. Morris, who summoned Shawn into the principal's office to bawl him out.

All this put him in a bad mood. And a sarcastic remark to Samantha, his girlfriend, sent her to the washroom in tears. On top of it all, the pop quiz in English was really hard and his eye caught Bobby's paper. Realizing he was about to fail, Shawn copied some of Bobby's answers.

As he walked home from school, he seemed to hear the Devil sneer at him. "A fine Christian you are! Your big mouth always gets you in trouble, and you even cheat! You're pretty insignificant in this big world. Why do you even try to do what is right? You'd be a lot happier if you stopped this religious routine and just went along with the tide."

Shawn was about to agree with everything Satan said when Brett, a Terrific Teens staff worker, drove up alongside him, beeped his horn and rolled down the window. "I'm going out for a Coke," he said. "Do you want to come along?"

"Sure," Shawn responded, and jumped into the car.

"How are things going?" Brett asked casually.

Shawn decided to tell him everything. By the time he finished, his friend had found a parking place and they were walking toward the restaurant. Brett picked out a secluded booth and they sat down.

Brett's smile was reassuring. "Shawn," he explained, "the Devil treats all Christians the same way. But getting some facts straight will help you tremendously. First, you need to know that the Devil is already defeated. God threw him out of heaven and Jesus wiped him out completely by dying on the cross and rising again. But he acts like the resentful kid who knows that the 'dirt bike' will never be his, so he tries to wreck it to keep anyone else from ever riding it. Satan tried to be God and failed. So now he uses sin, which is really an agent of decay, to try to destroy God's children—the most precious thing God has."

Brett went on. "You are extremely important to God. The Devil knows this, so he'll do everything possible to mess up your life. Don't expect him to change tactics!"

The Devil *will* spread drudgery, disease, and decay wherever he can. He'll try to sneak a spoonful of sin into your relationships, your family life, your thoughts, or your recreation time. Satan loves sin because he wants to spoil God's creation. But you can *hate* sin!

You can stand against sin in the power of Jesus. You're not in this war alone. Christians all over the world are fighting along with you, and Jesus is your captain. Every victory you win, by the power of the Holy Spirit, is a point for God's team!

MEMORIZE

"Resist him, standing firm in the faith, because you know that your brothers throughout the world are undergoing the same kind of sufferings" (1 Pet. 5:9).

PICTURE THIS

PERSONALIZE AND READ OUT LOUD

I will resist the Devil because I put my faith in the fact that Jesus has already defeated him. I know that I'm not the only one facing trials and temptations. Other Christians all over the world are also objects of Satan's attacks.

PRAY THE VERSE, APPLYING IT TO YOUR LIFE

Dear God, help me to resist the Devil. I believe in you and your Word. I pray for _____ and _____ (other Christians who are also facing heavy temptations).

PRACTICE FOR THE GAME

Be ready for Satan's next attack by digesting this Scripture verse. Put it on a card so you can "munch" on it throughout the day. Next time the Devil tells you that you're the only one tempted, quote this verse to him.

CHAPTER 10

The World's Greatest Disappearing Act

It was Saturday noon, and Crystal sat down with her mom to eat a tuna fish sandwich and a bowl of soup. Her older sister, Bonnie, had left early that morning to attend a cheerleading clinic in the city, and her father had told them that he'd have to stay at the office until his urgent business was finished.

Crystal's mom flipped on the noon news just in time to hear this report: *A van full of cheerleaders from Westfield High crashed head-on with a train traveling at full speed at Carver's Crossing on highway 69 at 7:30 this morning. Eight girls were killed instantly. One is in critical condition at Lane's Medical Center.*

Crystal's mother began screaming hysterically. "It can't be true! It can't be true! My Bonnie, my Bonnie!"

Crystal instantly pictured her sister's bloody body, and began sobbing. Thoughts flooded in: *I'll never see Bonnie again. We'll never share our secrets. How can I ever bear to see Bonnie in a casket? God, how could you let such a thing happen?*

After the most horrible ten minutes of her life, it occurred to Crystal to call her father's office. Her father was out, and all she got was the familiar: "Mr. Barron is out of the office. Please leave a message and he will return your call." Between sobs, Crystal managed to say, "Come home. We think Bonnie's dead!"

When they could cry no more, Crystal and her mom

sat on the sofa, too stunned and too paralyzed to do anything.

A half hour later her father called. Hearing his voice, Crystal broke down again. Then somehow she managed to blurt out what they had heard on the news.

Her father was shaken, but said he'd check with the police for details. Fifteen minutes later he called back. "Crystal!" he soothed. "It's all a mistake. The girls in the accident were from *Washington* High. Bonnie's just fine. I was able to get through to her and I talked to her myself."

Crystal was so relieved that she cried again.

Later, she began to think about the teaching her pastor had given just a couple weeks before. He had said, " 'Satan's only power over people is through manipulation and deceit.'* We've read the book of Revelation and we know how the story of mankind ends. All true Christians are on the winning side and they'll go to heaven. Satan and his followers will be confined to hell for all eternity. Misery likes company, so the Devil spends twenty-four hours a day trying to make everybody think the Bible's not true, that Jesus won't save, and that it's easier to live for worldly pleasures. But if you know the truth—if you love and obey the truth—the Devil can't touch you."

To Crystal, this hadn't made sense. She'd always thought of Satan as a being with awesome power. She'd heard many times, "You can't fight the Devil in your own strength." But now she could see how powerful deception is and how easy it is to break free once you know the truth.

If the Devil can convince you that you're hooked on drugs, or alcohol, or illicit sex, or hot fudge sundaes, or spreading juicy gossip, you won't even try to get free. If he can persuade you that God doesn't love you, or that you've committed the unpardonable sin, or that everybody despises you, or that you're inferior, he's on his way to destroying you. Deception is a very powerful weapon and Satan uses it well. But lies evaporate when you fully know the truth and follow it. Jesus said it all: "Then you

---

*Charles Stanley, *Temptation* (Nashville, Tenn.: Oliver Nelson, 1988), 40.

will know the truth, and the truth will set you free" (John 8:32). Truth, not Houdini, has the patent on the world's greatest disappearing act. When you put the truth about your freedom in Christ to work, Satan has *got* to disappear!

MEMORIZE

"But the man who looks intently into the perfect law that gives freedom, and continues to do this, not forgetting what he has heard, but doing it—he will be blessed in what he does" (James 1:25).

PICTURE THIS

PERSONALIZE AND READ OUT LOUD

If I concentrate on God's truth, found in His Word, I get free of the Devil's deception. The *catch* is that I have to persistently put God's Word into practice, constantly review God's truth, and act on it daily. If I do all this, God will bless my life.

PRAY THE VERSE, APPLYING IT TO YOUR LIFE

Dear God, help me to exchange all the Devil's lies for the truth found in the Bible. Show me where I'm not putting your principles into practice. I ask you to bless me, but I understand that you can't unless I constantly put your Word into practice.

GIVE YOURSELF A HEART CHECKUP

Prayerfully ask God to show you areas in which, although you know what God says in His Word, you're walking in disobedience. List these along with the verse you're disobeying (e.g., "I can't stand Barb and I always avoid her" versus "Love your enemies"). Determine to put God's Word into practice.

CHAPTER 11

The War Might Last One Hundred Years—Or a Little Less

Shannon and her mother clashed on just about every-thing: Christianity, allowance expenditures, practice time for piano lessons, grades and even the care of Conrad their cat. Because she'd been a Christian only a few weeks, swear words still surfaced in her vocabulary once in a while. Since she now ran around with the "God Squad" at school, her old friends made fun of her—and she didn't like it.

Shannon longed to be a spiritual giant instead of a baby Christian. In her daydreams she saw herself as a self-assured lady, married to a very handsome Christian husband. Re-spected by everyone, she would never lose her temper, swear, argue, or shirk her responsibilities. "Life without temptation . . ." she thought. "That will be so wonderful."

Then she attended the banquet her church sponsored for all the ladies and teenage girls. A famous writer was the guest speaker. What she said completely shocked Shannon.

"I'm still learning more than I'm teaching," she began. "And I've been a Christian for forty-five years. Recently I went through one of the toughest tests of my Christian life. The Devil even tempted me in areas I thought I'd completely conquered years ago!

"You need to remember these facts," she went on. "First: Temptation is not sin. Second: Everyone—even the world's best Christian—is tempted. Third: You'll never outgrow temptation. The Devil loves to see mature Chris-tians fall, so he works overtime on them.

"Right now, some of you are wishing you'd stayed home because this isn't what you wanted to hear.

"But the good news," continued the lovely, gray-haired lady, "is that the person who has the power to win learns to love the fight!

"My husband is a great football fan. I watch the pre-game shows with him, and I think the guys who smile and say 'I just can't wait to get out there on the field' are *nuts*. Who in their right mind would volunteer to be tackled by some 300-pound football player? Or risk playing even one game? But these guys, unlike you and me, are trained for the competition. They're in good condition. And the joy of winning makes it all worth it.

"Just remember that Jesus in you is stronger than the Devil, so you can fight with joy and you can win."

The speaker continued. "I learned another thing watching football with my husband. Goals are usually made *yard-by-yard*. It is very unusual to see a guy catch a punt and return it seventy-five yards for a touchdown. Persistence, hard work, hanging in there, and never giving up the hope of victory is what wins football games.

"The Christian life is no different. Learn to start each day with this prayer: 'Lord, I get to run this obstacle course again today! Thank you that this is an exciting life and that what I do counts for all eternity.' My part is letting Jesus live the Christian life through me. This cooperation includes persistence, Bible study and prayer, letting God give you love for people you'd rather not bother with and confessing sin even when admitting what you did is embarrassing or costly. All along the way," she concluded, "you'll experience little miracles—God giving you genuine love for the guy you just couldn't stand, power to say no, the joy of discovering and applying a new biblical truth, and the peace that comes from genuine repentance and receiving God's forgiveness.

"The war might last a hundred years—or a little less. However, victory after victory on earth—not to mention joy forever and ever in heaven with Jesus—makes enlisting in the battle well worth your while!"

MEMORIZE

"You need to persevere so that when you have done the will of God, you will receive what he has promised" (Heb. 10:36).

PICTURE THIS

PERSONALIZE AND READ OUT LOUD

I need to keep on doing what is right, standing on God's Word, and resisting temptation, so that when I've done God's will, I'll receive the prize—victories on earth and a forever that's more wonderful than I can imagine.

PRAY THE VERSE, APPLYING IT TO YOUR LIFE

Dear Lord, help me to stick with it. Right now _____ and _____ are really hard for me. Thank you that you have great promises that will be mine after I have done your will.

DON'T GIVE UP THE SHIP

Make several copies of this verse and put them in key places—inside your locker door, on your desk, on the dashboard of your car, on the mirror, etc. As you constantly review this verse, decide that you'll persevere in faith and keep on doing the will of God until you win victories in the hardest area of your life.

Self-Examination

Part I. The Rules of the Game

ACROSS
2. The Devil often impersonates _____ .
4. The Devil is a pain with a _____ .
5. The Bible says I am dead to _____ .
6. If I resist the Devil he must _____ .
8. Object of the Devil's hatred: _____ .
9. Person who will not let you be tempted beyond what you can bear: _____ .
11. Person who can overcome every temptation with the power of Jesus living inside: _____ .
13. Prefix meaning away from: _____ .
15. Temptation is my _____ .
17. Temptation brings out what is really _____ .
18. Temptation designed to destroy the mind: _____ .
20. _____ Jesus live the Christian life in you.
21. Invention of Satan: _____ .
22. Spanish for pronoun I: _____ .
23. One of two weapons Satan has at his disposal: _____ .
25. The Truth will set you _____ .
26. Person who will benefit by knowing all of this: _____ .

DOWN
1. Temptation should drive you to _____ .
3. If any man is _____ Christ, he is a new creature.
6. Temptation usually involves something _____ .
7. Need to overcome temptation: _____ .
10. Satan's big weapon: _____ .
12. The Devil will always make _____ on us until we get to heaven.
14. Book you can study to pass temptation tests: _____ .

15. All of our lives we'll have temptation _____ .
16. _____ evil suggestions come from the Devil.
18. Person who must receive permission from God to tempt you: _____ .
19. The Devil gives you a bad thought and then tries to make you feel _____ .
22. Satan can't get to Jesus, so he attacks one of His most prized possessions, _____ .
24. _____ you let Jesus live through you, you can be victorious.

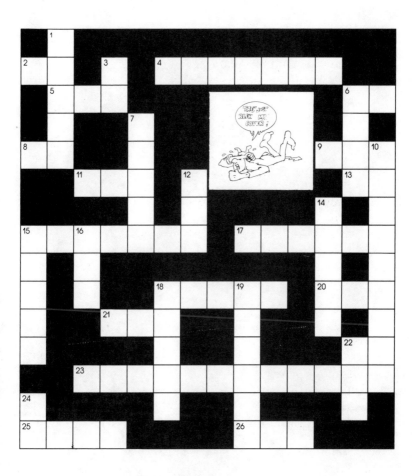

Answers are on page 189.

Part Two

The Best Defense Is a Good Offense

CHAPTER 12

When God Says, "Forget It."

Cristi had recently attended a special city-wide youth rally. The speaker made the Christian life seem so attractive that there was no way she could refuse his invitation to accept Christ as her personal Savior. After responding by giving her life to Jesus, Cristi experienced a joy and peace she'd never felt before.

It was just that—well, she thought once she became a Christian, she'd be *perfect* and all her problems would disappear. The new Christian friends she met at Bible study appeared to have it all together. But *she* still got D's on geometry tests. Although she tried a little harder, she hated cleaning the house as much as ever, and getting up in the morning was no easier than before.

One Saturday, her mother was in a particularly ugly mood. Halfheartedly, Cristi began to vacuum the living room rug. "I thought you were one of those saintly born-againers," her mother sneered. "Christians should work hard. You're the laziest thing I've ever seen! 'Cleanliness is next to godliness,' you know."

At this Cristi came out with a super-snotty barrage. She even used the name of Jesus as a swear word! Her mother returned with a ten-minute lecture, which could have been titled "Twenty-nine Reasons Why Cristi Is Good-for-Nothing." It ended with a familiar line: "Go to your room! I'd rather do the work myself than put up with such incompetence and lack of respect."

Alone in her room, her mother's accusations came at

her full force. That she was a hopeless case seemed like a foregone conclusion. She'd been through this syndrome before, but now she faced a new phenomenon. Other thoughts invaded her mind: "You've failed as a Christian. Don't ever expect God to forgive you. This sin is just too much for Him. Real Christians are made of stronger stuff."

At that moment, she heard her mother's voice from the bottom of the steps. "Somebody's here to see you." It was Debbie, the Bible study leader, dropping by to say that the study would meet on Thursday this week. But when she saw how discouraged Cristi looked, she gently asked what the problem was.

Breaking into tears, Cristi poured out her heart. Debbie listened sympathetically. Finally, she said, "I think we've been trying so hard to teach you kids how to live a victorious Christian life that we've forgotten something very basic. God forgives sin. Your first step is to apologize to your mother. Then, confess your sin to God and receive His forgiveness."

While Debbie stayed in Cristi's room praying, Cristi went to make amends with her mother. When she returned, they prayed together and Cristi asked God to forgive her sin. Afterward, she felt new and clean inside.

Opening her Bible, Debbie read Isa. 43:25: "I, even I, am he who blots out your transgressions, for my own sake, and remembers your sins no more."

Cristi smiled. It was really nice to hear God say, "Forget it."

MEMORIZE

"If we confess our sins, he is faithful and just and will forgive us our sins and purify us from all unrighteousness" (1 John 1:9).

PICTURE THIS

PERSONALIZE AND READ OUT LOUD

I will confess my sin of _____ . I will believe that God is fair and that He is faithful to forgive me and clean up my whole life.

PRAY THE VERSE, APPLYING IT TO YOUR LIFE

Dear God, I agree with you that _____ was sin, something horrible that stinks like garbage and must be thrown out. I believe that you're just and you always keep your Word. That means you totally forgive me and make me new and clean inside.

FORGET YOUR FAILURES

Make a list of the sins in your life that the Devil keeps reminding you of. After each one, write out 1 John 1:9 word for word. Then thank God for His forgiveness, burn the paper, and forget about them. God already has! And when the Devil reminds you of your past, remind him of his future!

CHAPTER 13

The Shack That Inferiority Built

Eric's hands were sweaty as he walked into the youth pastor's office. Although he knew that everyone in "Trinity's Terrific Teens" had been scheduled for an hour-long appointment with Pastor Dale during January, he felt nervous and wondered what he'd been doing wrong.

When Pastor Dale asked him to write down his three biggest problems, number one on his list was "an inferiority complex."

As the pastor asked some questions, Eric explained that his parents had been divorced when he was seven. His father had remarried and gone to live in another state. His mother then took a very demanding job and was hardly ever home. They rarely talked about anything important, or did anything together. When he was in junior high, his best friend had disappeared into the popular crowd, leaving him lonely and feeling rejected. In September he had started to date Julie and he really liked her a lot. But when Darren asked her to the Christmas banquet, Eric had been left behind in the dust. He didn't consider himself accepted by the youth group. Instead he stayed on the fringe.

He summed it all up, saying, "I guess I'm not good enough for anybody to really like a lot."

Pastor Dale looked at him with concern and compassion. "Eric," he began, "you've just swallowed one of the Devil's extra-strength formula lies—that you must base your life on the messages people have given you rather than on the truth of God's Word.

"Jesus likes you an awful lot, Eric. In fact, He loved you so much that He gave His life for you. His blood, which was shed for you, has more value than anything else in the whole world—and that's what you're worth. You're invaluable!" He quoted some neat scriptures Eric had never really thought about before:

> I have loved you with an everlasting love; I have drawn you with lovingkindness. I will build you up again and you will be rebuilt. (Jer. 31:3–4)
> This is love; not that we loved God, but that he loved us and sent his Son as an atoning sacrifice for sins. . . . God lives in us and his love is made complete in us. . . . God is love. . . . There is no fear in love. But perfect love drives out fear. (1 John 4:10–18)

"Eric," the pastor went on, "it's tremendously important that you believe what God says and *not* what people seem to be telling you. Never forget these words: 'We live by faith, not by sight' (2 Cor. 5:7). God says you're awesome, fantastic, full of potential and custom-made to do a tremendous job for Him."

If you want to cash in on everything that He put into you when He created you, you *must* be rightly connected to God—the source of your power. If the Devil can convince you that you're inferior, you'll be attacked by self-pity, the temptation to show off, desires to build yourself up by tearing others down, the craving to take drugs or alcohol to kill emotional pain—any number of temptations.

Satan knows that if he can get you to believe you're unlovable and no good, all kinds of sins can easily spring up in this unhealthy soil. But the *Jesus-loves-me-so-I'm-okay* kid won't feel so sorry for himself that he'll eat five bags of potato chips during one TV show. The person who is totally certain of *God's acceptance* doesn't need to brag that he got an 87 on the physics test that Bruce failed. The teenager who has learned to enjoy God's love doesn't frantically seek attention in socially unacceptable ways.

You, like Eric, have the opportunity of building a solid wall against temptation by accepting the fact that God loves you totally, completely, unconditionally, and forever. God loves you and that means you are lovable. He has accepted you, and that makes you acceptable. Period! Stop living in the shack that inferiority built, and move into the *God-loves-me-and-thinks-I'm-terrific* penthouse!

MEMORIZE

"As the Father has loved me, so have I loved you. Now remain in my love" (John 15:9).

PICTURE THIS

PERSONALIZE AND READ OUT LOUD

Jesus loves me just as much as God loves Him, and that's an awful lot! I must remain in His love by remembering that I have great worth because He loves me. I won't leave His love by swallowing the Devil's lie that when another person rejects me, it means I'm unlovable.

PRAY THE VERSE, APPLYING IT TO YOUR LIFE

Dear God, thank you that Jesus loves me just as much as you love Him—that I can be part of a family of love. Help me remain in this love. Keep me from receiving messages of rejection and deciding that nobody loves me—not even you.

WIPE OUT LIES ABOUT REJECTION

Make a list of the messages of rejection you've received in your life (e.g., "My sister always acts superior to me," "My math teacher laughed at me and called me a dumb blond"). With a red pen, write out all the words of John 15:9 over the rejection message and say out loud: "I don't believe this rejection message. I believe God loves me and that I'm valuable because Jesus paid such a big price for my salvation."

CHAPTER 14

It's Time to Stop Playing
Little Orphan Annie

Emily's father was drinking heavily again. And the line he gave about being laid off really meant that he had been fired from another job. Her mother held down a full-time job in order to support Emily and her four younger brothers. This meant that Emily did most of the housework, *plus* working Saturdays and keeping up with her schoolwork. She held a lot of resentment against her father. She also wondered why God allowed such a situation to exist in her family.

Emily had accepted Christ at a Bible camp when she was ten years old. But she never considered herself a very good Christian. She went to church every Sunday, but somehow felt as if she never lived up to God's expectations. Deep inside, she thought that God was just about as unfair as her earthly father.

When Blake, the guy she had liked for over six months, asked her to a play, she looked over her wardrobe in dismay. With Saturday's paycheck in hand, she went to the mall to buy something for the special occasion. Looking through the sale rack, she found the perfect dress—it even went with her best shoes! After trying it on and admiring herself in the mirror, she knew that nothing else would do. When she glanced at the price tag, she was *horrified*.

Desperation seized her. Why couldn't she have a father who could hold down a regular job and keep the family out of constant economic crisis? If only she didn't have so much responsibility at home, she could work enough to buy the things she wanted!

Looking at herself in the mirror once more, she was overcome with longing for the dress. *Everything* depended on this date with Blake! She just *had* to look great.

Suddenly, it occurred to her that the dress would fit nicely in the grocery sack, under the cornflakes, apples and laundry detergent she'd picked up for her mother. *If life weren't so unfair,* she reasoned, *I'd never have to do this.*

And so she tucked the dress neatly into the bottom of the sack, waited until the clerk turned her attention to another customer and walked out of the store.

It's easy to see that Emily fell into temptation because she had never come to the point of knowing God as her Father—a Father who loves and accepts her and wants to supernaturally care for her by meeting her every need.

Emily never even *thought* of praying and asking God to give her a nice dress for her date. It never occurred that she could trust God for Blake's response even if her outfit wasn't stunning. She just assumed that she was on her own and had to fend for herself.

Do you ever feel that way?

It's easy to picture God in terms of human fathers and other authority figures, instead of really receiving Him for who He is by faith. Sure, in your *head* you know that God can supply your every need. But do you know it in your *heart*? Do you live as though it were true?

A little child is never insecure in the arms of a loving father. You must learn that you can literally live in the arms of your loving heavenly Father. You don't have to search frantically for love. Just receive it from Him, and ask Him to give you good Christian friends to supply you with human love. Don't worry about all the things you don't have. Ask your heavenly Father for contentment and then pray for the things you need.

You don't have to feel forgotten, depressed and lonely. Your Father is always there, waiting to take you in His arms. It's time to stop playing "little orphan Annie" and start getting to know your Father, the best Father in the whole world.

MEMORIZE

"And God is able to make all grace abound to you, so that in all things at all times, having all that you need, you will abound in every good work" (2 Cor. 9:8).

PICTURE THIS

PERSONALIZE AND READ OUT LOUD

God wants to give me favor, love, and mercy. I can receive all I need and have plenty left over to share with those around me.

PRAY THE VERSE, APPLYING IT TO YOUR LIFE

Dear God, help me to constantly see you as the Father who always has for me all I need. I promise to start treating you as my loving Father, asking for the necessities of my life and expecting you to answer. Right now I'm asking you for _____ and _____ . I realize that the reason you give to me is so that I can help others.

OVERCOMING THE "ORPHAN" MENTALITY

List the ways in which you have been acting like an orphan (e.g., "I worry about what I'm going to do after graduation," "I keep complaining that no one understands me"). Next, write out how you would act in each situation if you *really* believed God was your loving and all-powerful Father. Take steps toward living like God's true child.

CHAPTER 15

The Devil's Best-Selling Fiction Isn't Fit to Read!

Tyler handed the report card to his mother. He anticipated the reaction that three C's and three D's would evoke. And he was not disappointed.

His mother scowled. "Why can't you be like your older brother? *He* always does his homework. *He* studies for each test and *he's* responsible. *He* doesn't constantly lose things, procrastinate, and conveniently forget about the work he promised to do. I don't know what to do with you."

That night, Tyler attended the second Youth League officers' meeting. Evan, the president, had made all the plans for the annual ski retreat in the mountains. He asked Tyler, who had just been elected treasurer, for the list of members who had paid the $20 reservation fee. At first, Tyler lied and said he had left the list at home. When the youth pastor insisted on taking him home to get it, he admitted that he had lost it. Under further questioning, he confessed that he couldn't remember who had paid him and that he had neglected to keep the money separate from his own—so he didn't really know the exact amount. This was too much for the youth pastor who gave him a half-hour sermon on faithfulness, using Evan as an example of a responsible person.

Tyler, a new Christian, felt like a total failure. Furthermore, he became convinced that God, also, compared him unfavorably with His other children. God was probably sick and tired of him. He was pretty sure that he had

70

tried God's patience to the limit and that God didn't want him anymore. He decided he really wasn't "Christian material" and that he might just as well give up.

Have you ever felt like that? The Devil tries very hard to make you (and every other Christian) believe that God doesn't love you anymore. Satan knows the person who feels that he or she has been abandoned by God will easily fall for any number of temptations. If the Devil can make you live by *feelings* instead of by the *fact* of God's Word, he's got you in his trap.

Never build your theology on how others have treated you, or on your emotions. Let God's Word be your only yardstick for truth. God has said:

> Never will I leave you; never will I forsake you. (Heb. 13:5)
> My sheep listen to my voice; I know them, and they follow me. I give them eternal life, and they shall never perish; no one can snatch them out of my hand. (John 10:27–28)
> . . . surely I am with you always, to the very end of the age. (Matt. 28:20)

God doesn't "robotize" His sheep and keep them in cages so they can't escape. Instead, He gives us free wills— and so much security and love that we will want to follow our Good Shepherd. But the Devil tries to obscure this *fact* with his *fiction*—that God doesn't love people who make mistakes, or act irresponsibly, or have bad breath.

Listen to the facts! God offers you total security. He always loves you. He never gives up on you. He will never leave you or forsake you. He is ready to forgive you and to create in you a clean heart. The Devil's best-selling fiction—that God has just given up on you—isn't fit to read!

MEMORIZE

God has said, "Never will I leave you; never will I forsake you." So we say with confidence, "The Lord is my helper; I will not be afraid. What can man do to me?" (Heb. 13:5–6).

PICTURE THIS

PERSONALIZE AND READ OUT LOUD

I believe God, not the Devil. And God has said He'll never leave me or forsake me. God has not given up on me. I say with confidence, "The Lord is my Helper." I'm not afraid of the rejection people hand me. It's God's opinion of me that matters.

PRAY THE VERSE, APPLYING IT TO YOUR LIFE

Dear God, thank you so much that you'll never leave me or forsake me. Thank you that you'll always help me, so I don't have to be afraid of people. If I'm under your protection, they can't do anything to me.

REPLACING FEELING WITH FACT

Write down the things you dread this week. Copy down this verse and keep meditating on it so you remember to use it to give you courage when one of these difficult situations arises.

CHAPTER 16

Discover and Attack One of the Devil's Favorite Sins

Doug was sitting in church with his parents—but he was doing everything possible to avoid listening to the sermon. He daydreamed of hitting a grand-slam homer. He tried to name the first ten presidents in order (figuring you could never study too much for one of Mr. Benson's tests). He planned the next fishing trip with Bill.

In spite of all this, he heard the pastor's piercing words: " 'Go into all the world and preach the good news to all creation' (Mark 16:15). This is obviously a command to every Christian. And God doesn't give any commands that He won't help us to fulfill. Those eleven disciples who first heard these words didn't evangelize the known world in a few years all by themselves. They had the help of almost every believer."

These words hit Doug as a condemnation, because he refused to believe that God could help him share Christ with others. Some people could witness, but he couldn't. You see, other people didn't stutter. Other people weren't naturally shy, and other people didn't break out in a cold sweat when forced to try to say something to a stranger.

As the pastor went on, Doug's mind went back to Friday's disaster. He had stood up in front of the English class to give his speech. When he couldn't get a word out, the compassionate teacher had asked him to come in after school to give her the speech privately. Even then he had stuttered and stammered, until he broke into tears of frustration. Repeated failure had left him feeling inadequate and inferior.

His thoughts were again interrupted by the pastor. "When Moses said he couldn't speak, God didn't say, 'How pious and humble! You poor thing. I can't really expect *you* to speak.' No, He got angry. I couldn't understand this for a long time," the pastor said, "but now I see that Moses' sin was the sin of *unbelief*. Moses didn't believe God when He promised to teach him how to speak. He considered God to be a liar on this point. That is very dangerous. Furthermore, he didn't believe that God could change him. He chose to accept past failure and present problems as fact rather than the Word of God—and he paid a big price for his choice.

"Unbelief," the pastor continued, "is one of the Devil's favorite sins. It's so subtle that most Christians don't even recognize it. If you steal, or commit adultery, or hit your brother, it's rather obvious that you're off track. But if you simply say, 'I believe my experience and my feelings instead of God's Word,' it seems rather innocent. But really, lack of faith is a terrible sin.

"The Bible says, 'Everything that does not come from faith is sin' (Rom. 14:23). If you don't believe that Jesus' blood can cleanse your sin, you won't get to heaven. And we never say, 'Poor Betty. She just can't believe that Jesus died for her.' That's because we know she can *choose* to believe. You *can* believe this promise: 'Therefore, if anyone is in Christ, he is a new creation; the old has gone, the new has come!' (2 Cor. 5:17). You can let God change you—or you can sin by lack of faith and stay exactly the same. You can decide to put your faith in this truth: 'And we know that in all things God works for the good of those who love him' (Rom. 8:28). Or you can worry about every detail. You can base your life on, 'The Lord is with me; I will not be afraid. What can man do to me?' (Ps. 118:6). Or you can become paralyzed by fear."

Finally the light flashed on! Doug realized that his unbelief was sin. He had believed the Devil's lie. It *was* possible for him to speak. God could perform a miracle in His life. If he didn't expect "instant pudding" but persisted in faith, God would free him from his fear of speaking.

When Doug left church that morning, he knew he had fallen for one of the Devil's favorite sins, the one that keeps people out of heaven and prevents Christians from realizing their full potential—the sin of unbelief.

MEMORIZE

"And without faith it is impossible to please God, because anyone who comes to him must believe that he exists and that he rewards those who earnestly seek him" (Heb. 11:6).

PICTURE THIS

PERSONALIZE AND READ OUT LOUD

Every time I show lack of faith, I let God down. I must believe that God is there—loving, all-powerful, and willing to solve every problem—and that He'll give me the answer I need if I keep looking to Him without giving up.

PRAY THE VERSE, APPLYING IT TO YOUR LIFE

Forgive me for the terrible sin of unbelief. Forgive me for becoming desperate about _____ and _____ , and not trusting you to resolve these problems. Forgive me for being a practicing atheist and looking in other places for my answers instead of seeking you with all my heart.

UNMASKING UNBELIEF

List pressure points in your life—areas where you're not really trusting God (e.g., "I don't really trust God to give me the dates and the social life that are right for me," "I worry constantly about my parents splitting up"). For two weeks—or as long as is necessary—specifically commit each of these problems to God every day, telling Him that you'll trust Him to take care of the situation and that you'll rest in Him.

CHAPTER 17

Get Off the Roller Coaster

Bridget spent an awful lot of time daydreaming about "Mr. Wonderful." She looked forward to the day she would fall in love, get married, and live happily ever after. Her greatest fear was becoming an "old maid." How she envied the girls who had steady boyfriends. *They* were assured of a date every Saturday night, got flowers on Valentine's Day, and had that special someone hanging around their lockers between classes. To her the word "boyfriend" spelled significance, security, success and the admiration of other girls.

When Allen asked her to the football game, she never even thought of saying no. Although she knew he wasn't a Christian and didn't have a flawless reputation, he *was* cute, popular, and a lot of fun. Being the center of his attention was the ego trip she had always dreamed of.

Before long, they were dating regularly. *And* before long, Bridget found out that Allen was very persuasive. Because her whole self-image was tied up in him, she always gave in. First it was drinking—just a little, to keep him company. Then it was petting and ignoring his bad language. Finally it was having sex with him.

Even though she felt guilty when her Sunday-school teacher came to her home to warn about the dangers of dating a non-Christian, Bridget just couldn't give him up. In spite of her fear of getting pregnant, she thought that saying no would mean losing Allen, and she didn't want to run that risk! It was easier to stay home from church than to go and feel convicted of her sin.

Allen became her whole life.

Are you a Bridget, caught in a similar sin syndrome? Charles Stanley, in his book *Temptation*, says something that's very important for you to know: "As long as men and women seek to gain their sense of significance and self-worth from anything other than God, they will set themselves up for temptation. . . . Until they change their definition of significance and until they transfer their security to Someone who can give them real security, they will never experience victory in their lives."

Have you bought into a lie from Satan? Do you equate significance with being a great athlete, dating pretty girls, getting good grades, or driving a sports car? Do you think security comes from having a steady boyfriend, being popular at school, or singing solos in the choir?

The only way to build a fortress that Satan can't penetrate is to get *all* your security and significance from God. Then you won't fall apart when you receive that "Dear John" letter. Not making the team, or getting a D on that test won't open the door for the Devil to tell you you're no good. If Jesus is *everything* to you, you won't be tempted to compromise your Christian principles for anything or anybody, because nothing will be *that* important to you.

If you permit Jesus to give you real significance and total security, you'll be able to get off the roller coaster and start traveling on the King's highway!

MEMORIZE

"It is because of Him [God] that you are in Christ Jesus, who has become for us wisdom from God—that is, our righteousness, holiness, and redemption" (1 Cor. 1:30).

PICTURE THIS

PERSONALIZE AND READ OUT LOUD

God has placed me, _____ , in Christ Jesus. And Jesus is everything to me: my wisdom, my guide for right living, my holiness and the One who paid the price for my salvation.

PRAY THE VERSE, APPLYING IT TO YOUR LIFE

Dear God, thank you that you put me in Christ. Forgive me for trying to fend for myself when Jesus is all I need. Show me how to find all my security, all my sense of value, all my wisdom, and all my righteousness in Jesus.

MEDITATE ON SCRIPTURE

Copy 1 Cor. 1:30 on to a card and review it many times during the day. Let this verse become part of you. As you go to sleep tonight, repeat the words of this verse.

CHAPTER 18

Who's a Hypocrite?

When Nathan started dating Kara, the only thing he could see was a vivacious, pretty girl who was considerate and caring.

As he got to know her, though, he noticed some negative qualities. Kara camouflaged her laziness with impossibility thinking. Whenever she faced a disagreeable task, Kara simply said, "I can't because I don't have time." Or, "I'm too tired." Or, "I don't know how to do it very well." If someone irritated her, she made no effort to hide her displeasure. It was obvious that there were some people she just couldn't stand.

One day, Nathan showed up at her house 45 minutes late because of an unavoidable traffic jam. Kara gave him the silent treatment. This was just too much for Nathan. He exploded. "You're one of the biggest hypocrites I've ever seen!"

Kara quickly rediscovered her voice and shouted back, "Hypocrite? What do you mean? I don't just pretend I feel loving if I don't. I don't act as if I want to do something when I'd rather not. I might not be perfect, but at least I'm *genuine.*"

Nathan recovered his cool and apologized. Then he began again, evenly, "Kara, what I'm going to say is very important, and I really want you to listen. You're a Christian and you're a new creature because the Bible says you are. As a believer, you are to accept what God says is true, not what you feel. If the Bible says, 'I can do everything through him who gives me strength' (Phil. 4:13), then you'd better think twice before you say 'I can't.' If Scripture instructs us to love our enemies and to forgive as Christ has forgiven us, that's truth—not your feelings of resentment or disgust."

Kara was stunned. She'd never thought of it *that* way before. But she saw that Nathan was right. She believed her feelings instead of the truth of God's Word.

The dictionary—and the Bible—define *hypocrite* as a person who plays a part or who pretends to be what he or she is not. The Devil's definition of a hypocrite is one who acts differently from what he or she feels. If some married man said, "I don't feel married, so I'll ask my secretary for a date," no one would applaud him for being "honest." He's totally deceived.

It's the same with you, a sincere Christian. Because Jesus lives inside you, you've got the power to do the things you dislike doing. So saying "I *can't* because I don't *feel* like it" is being a hypocrite. Jesus *can* love through you—to the extent that you really do love your enemies. You are a new creature in Christ, with the capacity to love everyone. That's the fact. Living according to your emotions and deciding to hate, or punish, or ignore a person who doesn't suit you is being a hypocrite, because you're just not living like the new you.

Are you trapped, like Kara? Do you obey your parents only when you feel like it? Do you put off doing things you don't like to do? Is your love reserved for those who measure up to your standards? Do your feelings control your "mood barometer"? Who's acting a part that doesn't fit? Maybe it's you!

MEMORIZE

"My purpose is that they may be encouraged in heart and united in love, so that they may have the full riches of complete understanding, in order that they may know the mystery of God, namely, Christ, in whom are hidden all the treasures of wisdom and knowledge" (Col. 2:2–3).

PICTURE THIS

PERSONALIZE AND READ OUT LOUD

I receive God's encouragement and I guard the unity I have with other Christians. I long to know more of Christ. In Jesus and His words recorded in the Bible, I'll find *all* wisdom and knowledge. What He says is truth no matter what my emotions tell me.

PRAY THE VERSE, APPLYING IT TO YOUR LIFE

Dear God, encourage me! Give me love for other Christians. Teach me more and more of Jesus. I promise to seek all my wisdom from Him and to live by His truth, not my feelings.

TRUTH OR CONSEQUENCES

Ask God to show you where you follow your emotions rather than His Word. List these areas along with the consequences of letting your emotions reign. Also indicate the actions and consequences of following God's commandments.

Self-Examination

Part II. The Best Defense Is a Good Offense

1. If you sin again, you are no longer a Christian.   T   F
2. If you sin, you should:
   _____ a. Confess it to Jesus.
   _____ b. Feel bad about it for a long time and do something good to cover it up.
   _____ c. Apologize, or in some way pay back what you have taken.
   _____ d. Accept God's forgiveness and go on in victory.

3. Your value is determined by:
   _____ a. How good your grades are and how well you perform.
   _____ b. How popular you are.
   _____ c. How many true friends you have.
   _____ d. How much God loves you and the high price He paid to redeem you.

4. If you *really* believe God is your all-loving and all-powerful Father:

_____ a. You'll know that you're always accepted by Him.

_____ b. You'll know that He'll supply what you need.

_____ c. You'll accept His discipline realizing it's best for you.

_____ d. You'll obey Him without reservation.

5. How does God feel about you?

_____ a. He's just given up on me.

_____ b. He'll give me one last chance.

_____ c. He loves me and offers forgiveness and a new start as I cooperate with Him.

_____ d. God helps those who help themselves.

6. What's wrong with saying, "I believe my experience instead of God's Word"?

_____ a. It's putting your trust in the mirages around you instead of in unseen reality.

_____ b. It's really saying that God is a liar.

_____ c. It forces you to operate on false assumptions.

_____ d. It makes you look to people for acceptance instead of to God.

7. If your sense of significance or importance comes from something or someone other than Jesus:

_____ a. You'll set yourself up for temptation.

_____ b. You'll do anything just to please that person or to obtain that goal.

_____ c. Pleasing Jesus won't be your only purpose in life.

_____ d. You must put that person or thing "on the altar of sacrifice," or you'll never be happy in your Christian life.

8. Which of these areas are weaknesses in your life?
   _____ a. Assurance of salvation and forgiveness.
   _____ b. Confidence that God loves me and that He is working through me.
   _____ c. Treating God as a loving Father, who will supply my every need.
   _____ d. Knowing that God will never give up on me.
   _____ e. Believing God's Word instead of my experience.
   _____ f. Getting all my self-worth and significance from Him.
   _____ g. Living by faith, not by feelings.

9. Ask God how you can build up these weak areas, and write down the ideas that come to mind (e.g., confession of sin, deeper surrender to God, memorizing Scripture to reinforce certain truths, listing the lies the Devil has been telling you and determining not to believe them).

10. Using the devotionals in Part II, list all the foundational truths that will help you build a strong wall to keep out temptation.

---

1. F. 2. a, c, d; 3. d; 4. a, b, c, d; 5. c; 6. a, b, c, d; 7. a, b, c, d; 8.–10. Personal.

Part Three

It's About That Hole in the Defensive Line

CHAPTER 19

Fighting—Without the Facts

"How 'bout a ride?" Dustin asked Joe one evening after the youth meeting.

"Sure," replied Joe. "Jump in. This here taxi is free."

Dustin climbed in Joe's old Ford. As they drove away from the youth center, he asked, "Was *everything* you said in that testimony of yours true?"

"Of course—do you think I'd lie?"

"We're old friends, right? And I know you're one of the world's most accomplished liars! Remember the time you convinced our geography teacher that your mother was dying? She felt so sorry for you she passed you, even though you didn't do any work!"

"But that was before I was a Christian," Joe countered. "Jesus has changed my life."

"Be honest now. Haven't you smoked even *one* joint lately?" Dustin persisted.

"No—not even one," Joe said firmly.

Dustin shook his head. "How do you *do* it? I have a constant struggle, and I've given in a couple of times recently. I'm about ready to give up on Christianity and go back to drugs. The craving just won't go away."

Joe pulled off the street into a supermarket parking lot and stopped the car. "Dustin," he began, "I don't think you really understand what happened to you when you gave your heart to Jesus. Something I just read might help you. Do you know how elephants are tamed?"

Dustin grinned. "This is a trick question, right?"

"No, I'm serious," Joe came back. "Just listen to this. When they want to tame an elephant, they tie him down so tight he can't even move. They don't give him anything to eat, and for days he struggles and thrashes around trying to get free. They even torment him to reinforce his feeling of helplessness. Finally, the elephant gives up. His will is broken to the extent that he can be tied to a little stake by a rope and he won't try to pull away. He doesn't even know the difference.

"Before Jesus came to live in our lives, neither one of us could get free from drugs. I tried and tried. I was like that tied-up elephant. But now the chains of sin have been removed. I still have the same emotions, the same thoughts and desires as before. Sometimes I don't feel free. But I don't live by my feelings anymore. Feelings lie."

Joe went on to explain that the power of sin is all around us, putting up paper tigers that look terribly real. We're used to responding to those "tigers" in certain ways. But the fact is, we *are* free. What the Apostle Paul said is true about each one of us. "I [that sinful me that likes to sin] have been crucified with Christ and I no longer live, but Christ lives in me. The life I live in the body, I live by faith in the Son of God, who loved me and gave himself for me" (Gal. 2:20).

"Well, I guess if I'm crucified, then I'm a dead man," Dustin said thoughtfully.

"For sure," Joe agreed. "And a dead man doesn't want to do drugs anymore. It's just that you have an outer shell—a body, mind, will, and emotions—that tries to demand certain things. The new you has the power to control those emotions and physical cravings by the power of the Holy Spirit who lives within you!"

You might as well know: The Devil wants this information to be a well-kept secret, because he hates people who are walking advertisements of the power of Jesus! He knows that he has a good chance of defeating the Christian who keeps fighting without the facts—and that he'll lose when we know the truth.

MEMORIZE

"Do not offer the parts of your body to sin, as instruments of wickedness, but rather offer yourselves to God" (Rom. 6:13).

PICTURE THIS

PERSONALIZE AND READ OUT LOUD

I was crucified with Christ, and so I'm dead to sin. Because of that, I, by the power of the Holy Spirit, can use my tongue for praising God rather than for gossiping, my feet to go on a walk with my grandmother rather than taking me to a place of temptation, and my eyes to read the Bible instead of watching a questionable program on TV.

PRAY THE VERSE, APPLYING IT TO YOUR LIFE

Dear God, thanks that I'm dead to sin and that, through the Holy Spirit, I have the power to offer the parts of my body to you and not to sin.

BEING THE BOSS OF YOUR BODY

Make a list of commands to give your body. Enforce them by the power of the Holy Spirit. For example:

1. Tongue, you'll stop criticizing _____ and find something good to say.
2. Mouth, you'll stop eating so much junk food and eat more vegetables.
3. Hands, you'll make the bed and clean the room before you play computer games.
4. Ears, you'll stop trying to hear the dirty jokes in the locker room and you'll listen more closely to the sermons on Sunday.

CHAPTER 20

Cliff Divers, Temptations, and Truth

Jillian was so excited she could hardly take it all in. Her family had planned this vacation for so long!

A big metal bird had lifted them from the snow and sleet of Chicago and set them down in the balmy paradise of Acapulco. The tranquil, bright blue of the horseshoe-shaped bay was breathtaking. A white sandy beach beckoned—and so did street-markets full of bright-colored clothes, tropical fruit, and an incredible variety of pottery.

Jillian's father, however, decided that the first thing on the agenda was a trip to watch the famous cliff divers that he had seen on TV. When they stepped out of the taxi, Lillian could hardly believe that anyone would jump from such a height into water so dotted with craggy rocks. But it was happening right before her eyes!

Concentration was the name of the game. Each action was slow and deliberate. These cliff divers didn't allow their minds to wander or give in to their emotions. They acted on fact: there was a way to jump safely and they knew how to do it with flawless precision. Inner fears, thoughts of landing on jagged rocks, and wrong information had to be totally discarded.

That night in her hotel room, before going to sleep, Jillian started reading Romans 6. Verse eleven caught her eye: "In the same way, count yourselves dead to sin but alive to God in Christ Jesus."

She also remembered her Sunday-school teacher's words. "When you accepted Jesus as your Savior, you became part of Him. That's what 2 Cor. 5:17 means by being 'in Christ.' At the same time His Holy Spirit came to live within you—'Christ in you, the hope of glory' (Col. 1:27).

"Because you are now one with Christ, everything that happened to Him happened to you. Maybe you don't clearly understand all this. But you can accept it by faith, because the Bible says it's true. 'For we know that our old self was crucified with him so that the body of sin might be rendered powerless , that we should no longer be slaves to sin—because anyone who has died, has been freed from sin' " (Rom. 6:6–7).

Jillian decided that considering herself "dead to sin" was much like those cliff divers who believed they could succeed—even though all common sense and natural feeling contradicted the truth. Now she could understand it! She had never really felt "dead to sin." In fact, temptations sometimes seemed overpowering. But that didn't change the facts: The Bible said she was "dead to sin," so that settled it.

Actually, she was living like a cliff diver who told himself "I can't do it" before each attempted jump. That's why Jillian kept yielding to temptations. She kept thinking: "I can't resist chocolate sundaes." "I just happen to be a critical person." "I was born moody." But now she realized that if she practiced keeping her mind on God's Word as much as those cliff divers trained their concentration on the ebb and flow of the tide, then the application of God's truth could change her.

That night—for the first time!—Jillian actually believed that constant victory over temptation was possible for her. She really could say, with the Apostle Paul, "We died to sin; how can we live in it any longer?" (Rom. 6:2).

MEMORIZE

"Set your minds on things above, not on earthly things. For you died, and your life is now hidden with Christ in God" (Col. 3:2–3).

PICTURE THIS

PERSONALIZE AND READ OUT LOUD

I can set my mind on Christ and the things of His kingdom—not on my fears, insecurities, and all the possibilities for sinning. Because the part of me that likes to sin was crucified with Jesus, this is not just mind over matter. It's believing and acting on the fact that my new nature, in Christ, isn't interested in doing wrong things.

PRAY THE VERSE, APPLYING IT TO YOUR LIFE

Dear God, help me to keep my mind on you. I will not think about _____ and _____ (present worries). Thank you that I died with Jesus on the cross and rose to live the new life He lives for me!

MEDITATE ON SCRIPTURE

Copy this verse on to a card and take it with you today. Spend the day with Col. 3:2–3 running through your mind, and fall asleep thinking about its message.

CHAPTER 21

Shopping, Surfing, and Romans 6

Although she was especially talented at sleeping in, Jillian found herself wide awake at 6:00 A.M. She jumped out of bed and peered through the drapes. Darkness covered the beautiful bay. This was a hotel room in Acapulco, and she couldn't just slip downstairs into the kitchen to rob the refrigerator.

Not wanting to wake her sleeping sister, she decided to take her Bible and escape to the bathroom.

There, by the light of the fixture over the sink, she looked up the verse she'd read the night before: "In the same way, count yourselves dead to sin but alive to God in Christ Jesus" (Rom. 6:11). She recalled watching the cliff divers who really considered themselves dead to feelings of fear, danger, and failure and focused on one simple truth: It was possible to jump safely. She had resolved to believe that victory over sin was possible because the Bible had said she was "dead to sin." She would believe God's Word instead of her feelings.

An illustration she had once heard came back to her. A chalk artist she'd met at home in Chicago had drawn a tree on his canvas. He said that the branches and fruit represented bad habits and fleshly response patterns in our lives—like anger, self-pity, revenge, and disobedience to authority.

"But instead of these bad branches," he had instructed, "we can engraft the truth of God's Word. When Bible verses become a daily part of our thoughts, wills, and emotions, they will actually become part of us. Then, the moment we're tempted, we can have the kind of victory over temptation that Jesus enjoyed."*

Jillian decided to start by memorizing and meditating on Rom. 6:11, determined to rely on that truth the moment she was tempted.

Later in the morning, out in the street market, Jillian found a gorgeous purple dress and just *had* to buy it— even though it meant parting with half of the spending money she'd brought. Returning to the hotel with her purchase, she met an American lady in the lobby who asked her how much she'd paid for the dress. When Jillian told her, the lady smirked. "You really got ripped off," she gloated. "Mine's exactly the same, and I paid one-third the price. You're still a 'gringa,' and don't know how to shop in Mexico."

To top it off, when Jillian got back to her room, she noticed a big spot on the skirt. Frantically, she tried to wash it out, but even the spot remover her mother had brought along failed.

Immediately, she became depressed and crabby. But after about twenty minutes, she remembered her morning's resolution. Quieting herself, she began to personalize Rom. 6:11, paraphrasing it: "In the same way, *Jillian* will count herself dead to *depression* and *moodiness* but alive to God in Christ Jesus." She repeated it aloud several times and let it sink into her spirit.

Then she realized that it was just like the Devil to try to convince her that a spot on a dress and losing some money was the end of the world. But because of taking a "Bible break" she conquered her depression.

Later, she totally enjoyed taking in the waves of the Pacific and eating exotic seafood in a tropical ocean-front restaurant.

That night she thanked God that His Word had rescued her from being bummed-out all day. She determined to

---

*Idea adapted from *The Eagle Story*, an Institute in Basic Youth Conflicts publication, 1984. Used by permission.

believe what God said about her. She decided to be just as diligent about engrafting Scripture into her life as the cliff divers were about their diving. It was amazing how Romans 6 related to shopping, surfing, and supper.

MEMORIZE

"We died to sin; how can we live in it any longer?" (Rom. 6:2).

PICTURE THIS

PERSONALIZE AND READ OUT LOUD

I died to _____ and _____ (recurring sins in my life). How can I live in them any longer?

PRAY THE VERSE, APPLYING IT TO YOUR LIFE

Dear God, thank you that I've died to sin. When temptation comes sneaking around, I just need to remember that the part of me that likes to sin is dead to sinful suggestions and can't respond to them unless I decide to jump out of God's protection and do my own thing. Thank you that I no longer need to live in wrongdoing.

NAILING IT DOWN

Put this verse on a card. Think about it constantly. Quote it to the Devil each time he tries to convince you that sinning is your only option.

CHAPTER 22

Stop Playing Tackle Football With Your Tongue

Cory's mom worked as a warden in a state correctional institution for women—and she was just as strict and unyielding at home as she was on the job. Cory's dad was a construction worker who drank, and they fought a lot. The one thing he learned from both of them was this: "It's a tough world out there, and you've got to learn to defend yourself."

Cory learned the lesson well. Even in first grade he had beat up a kid who called him names. When he couldn't use his fists, his tongue went into action. He earned titles like "Loud Mouth," "Smart-aleck," and "Tiger Tongue."

In his sophomore year, Cory met Wesley Whitfield. Wes was different from any friend he'd ever had. Although he talked about knowing Jesus, He was no sissy. In fact, he was the best player on the football team. He was self-assured, cool, and he really cared about Cory.

When Cory exploded because the officials declared the ball to be one inch short of a first down, Wes was the first to calm him down. When Cory was sent to the office for mouthing off to his English teacher, Wes took time to listen to his side and to talk things through. Wes asked him home for dinner; and everyone made him feel like part of the family.

Then Wes invited him to a Fellowship of Christian Athletes summer camp. Cory was delighted. At the camp he met many athletes who had put Jesus Christ first in their lives. And he decided to make Jesus his Lord, too. For the first time in his life he experienced unconditional love and a real sense of belonging.

Although his character changed in many ways, Cory still battled with his seemingly uncontrollable tongue. He blew up at Wes for arriving a half-hour late for their ski trip in the mountains. He criticized the youth pastor and made fun of his long nose. When Cindy suggested that he clean out his messy locker, he replied, "If Miss Perfect could get straight A's in chemistry like I do, I'd probably listen to her." Cindy burst into tears and walked away.

At times, Cory felt bad about his "Irish temper," but mostly he blamed others for not understanding him.

After an especially violent explosion of insults that Cory had directed at a church parking attendant, Wes decided to have a talk with him.

"Have you ever read Psalm 12?" Wes asked.

"I guess not," Cory admitted. "What does it say?"

"Why don't you read it?" Wes suggested.

Cory opened his Bible and started reading out loud: "May the Lord cut off all flattering lips and every boastful tongue that says 'We will triumph with our tongues; we own our lips—who is our master?' " (Ps. 12:3–4).

He shook his head. "I never knew *that* was in the Bible! I guess my big mouth is pretty disgusting to God, huh?"

"Cory," Wes continued, "God wants us to love and honor our parents. But sometimes they teach us things that aren't in line with His Word. I know your family, and your motto is something like, 'Tackle the other guy before you get knocked down yourself.' That's fine in football. But in real life a lot of innocent people get hurt. You can't blame your parents, because they were taught the same thing. Now that you know Jesus, though, you have to fall in step with His principles for right living. In fact, we all suffer tremendously from each lie we've received. Only the Bible is truth, and we gotta live by it."

The truth is this: It is not up to you to defend yourself. The Scriptures teach, "Do not take revenge my friends, but leave room for God's wrath, for it is written: 'It is mine to avenge, I will repay,' says the Lord" (Rom. 12:19).

The myth that you must be your own lawyer can lead you into all kinds of sins—criticism, anger, exaggeration, and false accusations, just to name a few. You need to learn to say, with David, "You are my refuge and my shield; I have put my hope in your Word" (Ps. 119:114).

So stop playing tackle football with your tongue, and rest in the fact that God loves you and cares about you. *He* will protect you.

MEMORIZE

"The name of the Lord is a strong tower; the righteous run to it and are safe" (Prov. 18:10).

PICTURE THIS

PERSONALIZE AND READ OUT LOUD

Instead of verbally attacking the person who hurt me, I will call on the name of the Lord. I'll let God put me into His tower, where I'll be perfectly safe.

PRAY THE VERSE, APPLYING IT TO YOUR LIFE

Dear God, _____ (name of person) said/did _____ , which really hurt me. Keep me from paying back evil for evil. Here I am, running to you and asking you to keep me safe in your fortress. Heal the hurts and make me strong again.

TAMING YOUR TONGUE

List the bad habits your tongue has gotten into, because of your fear that others will win and you will lose (e.g., putting down others to make yourself look good, repaying gossip with gossip). Then, after each item on your list write out the words of Prov. 18:10.

CHAPTER 23

Demolishing The Devil's Lie

Kelly felt as if her life were on a dimmer switch—and some unseen hand was slowly turning off the light. The people who mattered most to her seemed to form a chorus that chanted in unison, "Kelly, you can't. Kelly, you can't."

"Why don't you just get with it and bring home good grades like everyone else in the family?" her mother chided.

"Kelly, you drive like a scatterbrain, and I can't trust you with the car," her dad lamented. "If I let you loose on the streets, our insurance rates will double."

Her boss at Taco Bell fired her for inefficiency.

Her English teacher called her aside: "Kelly, your grades are a disaster. This theme is completely unacceptable. I'll give you two days to rewrite it or you'll receive a zero for the week."

On the day after her trip to the beauty parlor, all the girls giggled as she walked into homeroom. And Butch, the class loud mouth, said, "Where'd you get your haircut? In the poodle shop?"

The only bright spot in her life was Jack, her quiet, timid boyfriend. Other people laughed at him because he stuttered, but he understood Kelly and she adored him.

But then it happened. Jack informed her that he thought they depended too much on each other and that they should break up. That way, he explained, they would be forced to widen their circle of friends. To Kelly, this was the final blow.

"I'm a complete failure," an inner voice seemed to say. "Nobody loves me. I might as well kill myself."

Death seemed like the only escape. Because of what her church taught, she thought she'd go to heaven if she died, and that seemed a lot better than her horrible existence. Life seemed like an enemy, and death appeared to be her friend.

Kelly decided that taking a lot of sleeping pills would be the least painful way to go. She was just waiting for the right time.

Two days later, while Kelly was sitting alone at the school lunch table, Carla, the new girl in her class sat down beside her and put an arm around Kelly's shoulder. "Kelly," she began kindly, "you seem to be going through a rough time right now. Am I right? I want to be your friend. I'm here to tell you that Jesus can help you with your problems."

"It's too late," Kelly heard herself say. "I've already decided to commit suicide." She could hardly believe she was telling this to a complete stranger.

"Do you know who gave you the idea to kill yourself?" Carla asked.

"Nobody told me to," Kelly said dully. "I've just made my own decision."

"I'd like to read something to you from the Bible," Carla offered. "Listen to this: 'The thief comes only to steal and to kill and destroy; I have come that they may have life and have it to the full. I am the good shepherd' (John 10:10–11). Who do you think said this?"

"Jesus, I guess."

"Who do you think the thief is?"

"Probably the Devil."

"You're right. The Devil always wants death and destruction. But Jesus came to give us abundant life. Those ideas of worthlessness, depression, and defeat come straight from the pit. Satan loves suicide. In fact he even suggested that Jesus jump from the pinnacle of the temple, remember? But Jesus knew how to stand up to the Devil by using the truth of God's Word and rejecting all the Devil's lies.

Carla explained that Kelly needed to do two things: First, to invite Jesus to come into her heart to forgive her sins and run her life; second, to begin the process of building her life up in line with what God says is true, not according to the feedback she was getting from people, or on the thoughts the Devil was cramming into her head.

"Jesus loves you so much that He shed His blood on the cross to save you," Carla said. "His blood is the most valuable thing in the whole world. That means you're priceless to God.

"Just listen to this:

> 'For I know the plans I have for you,' declares the Lord, 'plans to prosper you and not to harm you, plans to give you a hope and a future' (Jer. 29:11).

"God really has a wonderful purpose for you. He made you special, to do something no one else can do. Don't build your life on your expectations or those of others. Let God teach you who you really are, a person of great value and great potential."

Suicide may never have been one of your temptations—or maybe it has! Whatever your situation, it is important that you recognize the Devil's strategy of death and destruction. Anything less than an abundant life full of hope, joy, peace, love, and all those good things means the Devil is stealing something from you. Don't just accept your feelings of worthlessness, inferiority, and frustration. You are valuable. You are loved. Whenever you forget that, the Devil is there with a variety of temptations—self-pity, self-hatred, suicide, blaming others, criticism—and the list goes on.

Don't frame the pictures of yourself that are handed to you by people who reject you. Fight the fight of faith—taking God's Word at face value and demolishing the Devil's lies!

MEMORIZE

"Whoever believes in me, as the Scripture has said, streams of living water will flow from within him" (John 7:38).

PICTURE THIS

PERSONALIZE AND READ OUT LOUD

I must believe in Jesus. Rather than feeling worthless, I will believe the truth: that because Jesus died for me, I am valuable. I choose to believe that He loves me as He said, instead of considering myself friendless. Then that fountain of living water, with its joy and peace, will spring up inside me.

PRAY THE VERSE, APPLYING IT TO YOUR LIFE

Dear God, help me to believe what you say in every situation. Right now I'm having trouble believing _____ . I chose to believe you and to permit those streams of living water to flow from within me.

MEDITATE ON SCRIPTURE

Copy this verse on to a card and take it with you today. At each opportunity repeat the words of this verse and apply them to your life. Go to sleep meditating on John 7:38.

CHAPTER 24

Idols, Baseball, and Christian Cardiograms

It was the bottom of the ninth. The score was tied 3–3. With two outs and runners on first and third, Brandon Williams knew that he had a chance to become a hero and to return the district championship trophy to Pinesville High.

After taking two balls, he swung at a perfect pitch—and thrilled to the crack of the bat. The ball sailed over the left-field fence!

As he rounded first base, he imagined a nationally known sports announcer shouting, "Going, going, gone! It's a home run!" He heard the fans going wild and savored the thought that this would not escape the notice of the Kansas City Royals' scout who was sitting in the stands.

When Brandon crossed home plate, his teammates mobbed him. The Pinesville Herald reporter took several pictures. Everyone in the stands was yelling, "Bran-don! Bran-don! Bran-don!"

From that moment on, Brandon became obsessed with the idea of becoming a major league star. Before, he'd thought of his baseball talent as a means of opening more doors to witness to others about his faith in Jesus. Now baseball became his life.

He stopped going to Bible study in order to attend a special pitching clinic in a nearby city. That summer he dropped out of youth group, because he played on three different summer teams and had no time for anything else.

When he started his senior year, Brandon sacrificed

everything for his goal: receiving the best available baseball scholarship. He even stayed home from church on Sunday mornings to study.

In itself, baseball is a good, healthy sport. It was Brandon's *attitude* toward it that became the spiritual problem. The Bible says, "Above all else, guard your heart, for it is the wellspring of life" (Prov. 4:23). Because Brandon didn't guard his heart, baseball became his idol.

When something becomes too important to you, the Devil can use it to tempt you to sin. If having all the right clothes is all you think about, Satan can suggest that you shoplift when you don't have the money to buy what you "need." If having free time to do exactly what you want is your priority, it's pretty easy to leave a job undone or to shirk responsibility. If your goal is straight A's no matter what, the Devil's suggestion that you carry a crib sheet to that super difficult exam sounds inviting.

Almost anything we find in the world could turn into a temptation—good food, sports, new cars, classmates. It all depends on your *attitude.* Don't ever blame your temptation on God by saying something like, "If God hadn't let that guy leave his keys in the ignition, I'd never have been tempted to steal the Corvette."

Be honest. The temptation came because you wanted something more than you wanted to obey God. The Lord allows us to face decisions like this, but His purpose is always that you say no to temptation and become stronger than ever.

Let God give you a heart check-up—a Christian cardiogram. Do you have some desires that are out of hand? Give them to God before they open the door to all kinds of temptation. Remember: "Above all else, guard your heart. . . ."

MEMORIZE

"For God cannot be tempted by evil, nor does he tempt anyone; but each one is tempted when, by his own evil desire, he is dragged away and enticed" (James 1:13–14).

PICTURE THIS

PERSONALIZE AND READ OUT LOUD

God can't be tempted by bad things, and He never tempts me to sin. It's my off-balance desires that create my temptation. (e.g., "Food is fine, but not if I want too much of it. An opportunity to steal can only be a temptation if my craving for things is out of control").

PRAY THE VERSE, APPLYING IT TO YOUR LIFE

Forgive me if I've ever blamed you for temptation. I acknowledge that my wrong desires are what lead me into temptation.

DEMOLISH DECEITFUL DESIRES

List the longings you have that can easily get out of hand. (e.g., "I want a girlfriend/boyfriend so bad that I can easily forget God in my campaign to impress a suitable candidate!) Every day for a month (longer if necessary), surrender each of these desires to God.

CHAPTER 25

Smart-Alecks Don't Pray, "Lead Us Not Into Temptation"

Chuck returned from Bible camp all fired up. He felt bold, powerful, and ready to conquer the world.

He and Brad decided to go to some parties with the old gang so that they could witness. When Brad called to say that his parents had grounded him, Chuck didn't give it a second thought. He pictured himself as the brave and fearless ambassador for Christ, who was immune to all the temptations of his former life-style.

When he arrived, Allison met him at the door. Her short-shorts and halter top caught him off-guard. But he thought, *No, I'm a strong Christian.* Inside, though, the smell of marijuana awakened in him an old craving. Then Jeannie—the girl he'd always wanted to date but whom he could never impress—rushed up to him. "It's time you came back to your senses! That Jesus-freak stuff is just for sissies. Come with me. I've got some really good coke."

All of a sudden, Chuck felt completely alone—abandoned by God and open to every temptation. The thought of witnessing never occurred to him. In fact, the desire to get high again was more than he could resist—especially since it also included special attention from Jeannie.

When he arrived back home at 2:00 A.M., he saw his Bible on his bed. Although his head was somewhat cloudy, he felt a tremendous sense of guilt. Slumping down on the bed, he tried to pray. The words that came out, automatically, were those of the Lord's Prayer, which he'd repeated every Sunday for years. When he came to "and lead us not into temptation, but deliver us from evil," he stopped short.

The next morning, when his brain cleared, Chuck wondered why Jesus taught his disciples to pray, "lead us not into temptation."

Then, suddenly, the answer occurred to him: Relying on his own strength, he had walked into Satan's trap and had gotten caught. He should have *expected* this outcome, because no human is a match for the Devil. He recognized that if he sincerely prayed "lead us not into temptation," it gave God permission to eradicate his pride and change other attitudes.

Vaguely, he remembered a special speaker saying: "A valid interpretation of this Scripture would be, 'Dear God, let there be nothing in my heart that would cause you to put me to the test.' "* His brash self-confidence had literally led him into temptation.

Chuck also acknowledged that some Christians he thought of as stodgy knew what they were talking about when they advised him to stay away from any place that had once been the scene of his sin. It was wrong to seek spiritual danger as a form of adventure.

Now Chuck knew that *he* could not be victorious over the Devil. He had to admit that he was weak and totally unable to resist temptation. He had to resolve that every time the Devil knocked, he would tell Jesus, "*You* go to the door." When Jesus faces Satan's temptation, He is victorious.

Jesus in you can resist sin. But only if you are not undermining yourself by placing yourself in tempting circumstances. If you disregard the advice of your spiritual authorities, and if you have a cocky confidence in your own righteousness, then the real prayer of your life is, "Lead me *into* temptation. Show me the way!"

Or is your true prayer, "Lead me not into temptation"?

---

*Bob Mumford, *The Purpose of Temptation*, p. 119.

MEMORIZE

"And lead us not into temptation, but deliver us from the evil one" (Matt. 6:13).

PICTURE THIS

PERSONALIZE AND READ OUT LOUD

I will ask God not to lead me into temptation and will help answer my own prayer by staying away from anything that looks like trouble. I will ask God to save me from the Devil, instead of being so cocky as to think I can face him by myself.

PRAY THE VERSE, APPLYING IT TO YOUR LIFE

Dear God, I ask you to guide me and keep me from walking straight into temptation. I admit I'll never be able to withstand Satan in my strength. Deliver me from His deception.

AVOIDING THE DANGER ZONE

Identify attitudes that could easily lead you into temptation. Allow God to change your way of thinking. In each problem area ask God to deliver you and erect walls of protection around you.

CHAPTER 26

What Ordering Yourself Around Has to Do With Overcoming Temptation

In the darkness of her room, Sara relived her day.

Her Saturday morning "sleep-in" had been disturbed by an emergency message: The house was in danger of becoming a pigpen if it were not cleaned immediately. Sara hadn't quite honored her mother. In fact she had protested and complained until her mother repeated her "ungrateful daughter" speech and gave in.

After lunch, April had invited her to go shopping. When they stopped for a diet Pepsi Sara took one look at the new giant sundae ad—and that was the end of her new weight-loss program.

Then she saw a dress she just couldn't live without, and convinced April to charge it on her mother's Visa card, even though she didn't know where she'd get the money to pay her back.

Arriving home, she flopped in front of the TV, feeling too exhausted to start on Monday's big assignment, or to return her overdue library books.

That evening when the youth group president asked her for a report on what her committee had done about finding a place for the Christmas banquet, she invented some "facts" that were totally untrue, rather than admit that she had done nothing at all. On the way home, she began to feel guilty.

Now, as the grandfather clock in the hall struck midnight, Sara's conscience gave no indication it was ready to retire for the night. *You claim to be a Christian,* that inner voice was saying, *yet you don't obey your mother. You don't exercise self-control. You aren't concerned about paying your debts. You're not a good student, and you even lie to cover up your laziness.*

She had to agree; her conscience was right. And she knew what she should do. She should apologize to her mother and clean the house next Saturday, return to her diet, take the dress back to the store and confess her lies to Jeff, the youth group president.

But at the same moment, another inner voice told her she just couldn't face all that suffering. Everybody would say she was terrible—and maybe it was true. She felt trapped and paralyzed. She didn't seem capable of doing one thing she didn't want to do.

The clock struck one and, mentally, she changed the subject.

Do you ever feel like Sara? Does your laziness, procrastination, and inability to deprive yourself of any small pleasure make you easy prey for Satan's temptations?

Only *you* can put discipline into your life. The book of 2 Peter tells us how to "escape the corruption in the world caused by evil desires" (2 Pet. 1:4). Part of the plan is this: "Make every effort to add to your faith goodness; and to goodness, knowledge; and to knowledge, self-control; and to self control, perseverance" (vv. 5–6).

What are some practical ways to add self-control and perseverance to your faith?

One way is to put Eccles. 9:10 into practice: "Whatever your hand finds to do, do it with all your might."

Attack the hardest homework assignment first. Mow the lawn now and relax later. Clean your room without being told. Practice obeying your parents without comment. Volunteer for jobs—even the hard ones—and do them well, offering them as a service to God. Be like Jesus, who washed His disciples' feet.

You don't have to give in to all your desires. Ask God what you should buy. Decide not to purchase anything you don't have the money to pay for, and obey Rom. 13:8: "Let no debt remain outstanding." Don't permit yourself to become a slave to food or any other physical desire. A good way to break the hold these desires have is by fasting.

"Wait a minute," you may be saying, "every red-blooded teenager needs to eat constantly. Fasting sounds like something people did 2,000 years ago."

Well, they did fast—and they loved their neighbors, preached the gospel and did a whole bunch of other things found in the Bible. Jesus was against fasting as a way to show off or to fulfill some kind of legalistic schedule, but He fasted himself—and so did Esther and Nehemiah and Daniel and Jehosaphat, and the church at Antioch. Do a Bible study on fasting. (By the way, it's good for your health! Usually, it's wise to start by skipping one meal and spending that time in prayer and Bible study.)

Building self-discipline will help you say no to the Devil's suggestions that you need constant comfort and self-indulgence. So really, ordering yourself around has a lot to do with overcoming temptation.

MEMORIZE

"Sin is crouching at your door; it desires to have you, but you must master it" (Gen. 4:7).

PICTURE THIS

PERSONALIZE AND READ OUT LOUD

The Devil will see to it that sin is knocking at my door. Right now the temptation to _____ is very strong. But I must master it, not only by saying no today, but by putting disciplines into my life to make me better able to resist in the future.

PRAY THE VERSE, APPLYING IT TO YOUR LIFE

Dear God, help me to always recognize the sin that wants to overcome me. Show me how to master sin, both by saying no today and by building self-control into my life.

DEVELOPING DISCIPLINE

List five areas of weakness in which you experience a lot of temptation. Pray and ask God what decisive actions you need to take and what character-building exercises you should engage in to reinforce this area of weakness. (e.g., If procrastination is your problem, clean off your desk *now*, and then make a list of unfinished projects and complete them one by one.)

CHAPTER 27

Are You a Christian Track Star?

When Jolene gave her heart to Jesus her life changed radically. She stopped hanging around with her old girl-friends, gave up drugs, and broke up with Dan. Making new friends wasn't easy, but she did it.

Although she was often faced with the desire to get high and had longings for sexual pleasure, the joy she discovered in Jesus was so wonderful that she never wanted to return to her old life. She experienced the power of the Holy Spirit giving her a new-found ability to say no. As the months passed, she became more firmly established in her Christian way of life.

But one Saturday night, it seemed as if Satan came to pay her a visit in person. Everyone else in her family had gone out for the night. The house felt lonely and deserted. The soft lamplight cast shadows on the walls, and Jolene sat on the couch trying to read a book. But she just couldn't concentrate.

Her Christian friends had let her down. She wasn't invited to Brenda's birthday party, and it hurt her deeply. Not only that, just that morning her mother had accused her of being "a religious fanatic—the only odd-ball in the family." Startled by a sudden noise, she felt that some unknown evil must be lurking in the shadows. Depression and fear descended upon her.

A few moments later, there was a knock at the door.

It was Dan. Smiling and good-natured as always, he began, "I miss you so much, I just can't stay away."

To Jolene he looked more attractive than ever—curly hair, athletic build, contagious smile—and the one person who'd thought of her on a lonely Saturday night. When he suggested they go out for a bite to eat at Burger King, she couldn't refuse.

It had been so long since anyone had told her she was pretty, and as they talked quietly that evening she soaked in all Dan's compliments. Listening to him say, "I love you," felt so comforting and so right. The desire to have Dan take her in his arms became overwhelming. It was like God and His ideas about right and wrong ceased to exist.

Getting into the car again, Dan drove to the bluff that overlooked the Mississippi. There, she enjoyed his physical closeness—and then she surrendered herself to him as she had done so many times before. She felt like a programmed robot with no power to resist.

Of course when she got home, she felt terrible. She cried and cried. She was sure that God didn't love her anymore and that there was no forgiveness.

On Sunday morning, Jolene decided not to go to church. But at nine o'clock, Shirley called to remind her that the youth group had planned a picnic after the service and that she was counting on Jolene to bring the soft drinks. It was only because of her strong sense of duty that Jolene assured Shirley she'd be there.

God used the Sunday morning sermon to show Jolene the way out of her predicament.

"Sometimes running away is the only means of resisting the Devil," the pastor was saying, "and you must run straight into the arms of Jesus. The Bible says, 'Flee from sexual immorality' (1 Cor. 6:18), and 'Flee the evil desires of youth' (2 Tim. 2:22). God's Word never says to stand up and face evil like a strong Christian. In fact the root of our problem with temptation is that we rely on something good and strong within ourselves—which just isn't there."

Keep out of the danger zone. Don't stop at your favorite ice cream parlor, thinking you'll only order a diet pepsi.

Stay miles away from a situation that will bring sexual temptation. Leave the house to avoid throwing a fit that's designed to manipulate your mother into giving you your own way. If a surprise attack takes you off guard, physically escape, as Joseph did.

God can seem far away when your mouth craves that chocolate sundae, your body longs for sexual experience, or your emotions insist on staging a tantrum. At that moment, look for the nearest exit and start running! You'd do well to become a Christian track star.

MEMORIZE

"Flee the evil desires of youth, and pursue righteousness, faith, love and peace" (2 Tim. 2:22).

PICTURE THIS

PERSONALIZE AND READ OUT LOUD

I will run away from _____ and _____ (evil desires I have). I will run toward right living, faith, love and peace.

PRAY THE VERSE, APPLYING IT TO YOUR LIFE

Dear God, show me other youthful lusts I should run way from. Make me hungry for righteousness. Instead of goals like having a girlfriend/boyfriend, being a sports star, or having a lot of sharp clothes, give me the desire to increase my faith, to grow in love and to receive your peace.

MAKE NEW GOALS

Ask God to give you one specific way to accomplish each of the following objectives. Write it down and prayerfully seek to put it into practice.

1. Flee youthful lusts _____ .
2. Pursue righteousness _____ .
3. Abound in love _____ .
4. Receive more peace _____ .

CHAPTER 28

The Decline and Fall of Practically Everybody

Joel was into being "Mr. Success." Ever since he could remember, he was taught, "Give it all you've got and be the best." When he pitched a good game in Little League, he'd loved hearing his dad say, "That's my boy!" If he got straight A's (which was most of the time), his mother would comment, "I've always wanted a son who excelled in academics, and you're my dream come true." To Joel, acceptance only came from achievement. He knew how to play the game and he played it well.

His senior year brought him a merit scholarship, he was voted "best all around," and he was chosen captain of the baseball team and the president of the youth league at church. His parents were proud. His girlfriend, Nicole, adored him. And he felt that God was pleased because he read his Bible every day and lived a good clean Christian life.

But in March everything started going wrong. A broken leg on his last ski trip wiped out his baseball season *and* his dream of leading the team to the state championship. His father's cancer surgery worried him so much that he couldn't concentrate and his grades started to slip. Nicole started dating Dave. Now that Joel couldn't perform the way he used to, he felt rejected by everyone. All of a sudden he felt helpless.

Slowly and painfully, Joel learned some important lessons. He had never really depended on Jesus to live the Christian life through him. He'd done all the right things, but he'd done them in his own strength. Now he had to depend on Jesus to keep some flaky freshman from knocking his crutches out from under him and sending him down the steps. He had to trust Jesus to take care of his father so he could concentrate on chapter eighteen in Physics. And he had to literally think about Jesus just to keep from falling apart when he passed Nicole and Dave in the hall on the way to English class.

Then Joel got his first C on a big test. He began to feel inferior to Dave. Watching the baseball game was pure agony. "Mr. Success" had vanished. Now Joel was struggling to keep his head above water. During this time, Joel took special notice of a verse he read in his Bible:

> And whatever you do, whether in word or deed, do it all in the name of the Lord Jesus, giving thanks to God the Father through him (Col. 3:17).

It struck him that there was no mention of doing everything right, or being the best. God's criteria was that he act in the name of Jesus through the power of the Holy Spirit for the glory of God. In other words, the Lord grades on motives, not performance.

Then he realized that getting a C while depending fully on Jesus, and giving the thanks to God, was better than getting an A through his own efforts. Watching the game with his mind on Jesus was obeying Him, while secretly taking all the credit for a grand slam home run was disobeying Him. Being acceptable to Jesus was the thing that mattered, not being Nicole's dreamboat.

Joel had fallen for one of the Devil's most subtle temptations—doing the right things with the wrong motive, sometimes called "walking in the flesh." He'd been so busy succeeding that he had no time to depend on God—until he had to.

If you don't want to be part of this "decline and fall of practically everybody" scenario, ask God to show you where you are depending only on your own strength.

Consciously ask Jesus to live through you as you do homework and eat pizza and watch television. Those who listen to God's still small voice don't have to be hit over the head with a ton of bricks.

MEMORIZE

"Those who live according to the sinful nature have their minds set on what that nature desires; but those who live in accordance with the Spirit have their minds set on what the Spirit desires" (Rom. 8:5).

PICTURE THIS

PERSONALIZE AND READ OUT LOUD

If I'm "walking in the flesh," my mind is on me—my pride, my reputation, my convenience, and my control of the situation. If I'm walking according to the Spirit, I'm thinking about how to let the Holy Spirit live through me and how to give glory to God.

PRAY THE VERSE, APPLYING IT TO YOUR LIFE

Dear God, keep me from setting my own goals, making my own decisions, and having my own way. Instead, help me always to be conscious of permitting the Holy Spirit to live through me. Keep my mind on you. Right now I want you to live through me as I _____ (complete this important task).

MEDITATE ON SCRIPTURE

Write this verse on a card to take with you today. Whenever you have a free moment, meditate on this verse. Go to sleep with its message on your mind.

Self-Examination

Part III. It's About That Hole in the Defensive Line

1. If I really died to sin, why do I have so much trouble with temptation?
   _____ a. It works for others but not for me.
   _____ b. The Devil did such a good job of chaining me before I became a Christian that my mind and emotions still don't think I can get free.
   _____ c. I don't try hard enough.
   _____ d. I'm fighting without the facts: Jesus set me free and the Devil can't enslave me anymore.

2. Which things are involved in "considering yourself dead to sin"?
   _____ a. Waiting until I feel "dead to sin."
   _____ b. Accepting it as a fact, because the Bible says it's true.
   _____ c. Living as if I'm "dead to sin."
   _____ d. Trying to understand it all with my mind.

3. Personalize Romans 6:11. In the same way _____ counts himself/herself dead to _____ and _____ but alive to God in Christ Jesus.

4. What lies do *you* live by? (Principles you've been taught that don't line up with God's Word.) _____
   _____

5. What's the Devil's strategy? D _____ and D _____ .

6. What is an idol? _____
   Is there any idol in your heart? _____
   What is it? _____

7. God can't deliver me from evil if:
   _____ a. I'm still a baby Christian.
   _____ b. I don't have devotions in the morning.
   _____ c. If deep down in my heart I have the kind of pride that insists on being the big hero.
   _____ d. If I don't know the Bible from cover to cover.

8. Pray and ask God what *you* need to do to build self-discipline into your live. Write these things down.
   _____
   _____

9. What is the best way of handling sexual temptation and other temptations of the flesh? _____
   _____

10. The Lord grades on motives, not _____ .

10. Performance.
8. Personal; 9. Avoid the danger zone and if caught off guard, start running;
6. Something that becomes more important to you than God; Personal; 7. c;
1. b, d; 2. b, c; 3. Personal; 4. Personal; 5. Death and Destruction;

Part Four
Hold That Line

CHAPTER 29

Deanna's Dilemma

Deanna, a high school senior, was completely swept off her feet by Scott, a handsome Texan who came to study pharmacy at the University of Michigan. He was part of a Christian singing group, and he owned an impressive library of Christian books.

Deanna soon learned that some of his ideas were unconventional, but he was so persuasive that she couldn't resist his line of reasoning. When her father raised some doubts about Scott's integrity, she flew to his defense. "Well, he's a much better Christian than the guys I grew up with at our church."

One day, Scott explained to her that he believed marriage was just a formality. After all, he said, Isaac just brought Rebekah to his tent and they started "living together." He thought that a marriage license was just a piece of paper and that "true marriage" was an attitude of the heart.

Then he declared his undying love for Deanna, and gave her a tour of the luxury apartment he'd just rented. "I looked until I found the perfect place for you," he cooed, "and I'm inviting you to move in with me."

Deanna had never thought of things that way before, but Scott's argument seemed so sophisticated and logical. Her heart clouded with doubt. Maybe the things she'd always been taught were wrong.

Deanna spent a sleepless night pondering every angle. Her mind became a fog of confusion and questions.

The next morning, Heather, the pastor's daughter, stopped by to pick Deanna up for school. She noticed that Deanna looked troubled, and asked, "What's the matter?"

"Well," Deanna replied, "I might as well be honest. Is it really *wrong* to live together without being married? Scott says that Isaac and Rebekah did it."

"First off," Heather answered, "you've got to remember that doubt is the Devil's introduction to temptation. If he can get you to doubt God's Word, the rest of his job is easy. No matter what the issue is, you have to decide that God's Word is true and that every argument contrary to the Bible is false."

But what about Scott's argument? What *does* the Bible say about marriage?

It's important to understand that marriage laws in the nomadic tribes of which Isaac and Rebekah were a part consisted of an arrangement made between the parents of the man and woman. Modern marriage laws are different. God doesn't look at a marriage license as just a piece of paper, because Prov. 28:9 tells us, "If anyone turns a deaf ear to the law, even his prayers are detestable."

The Old Testament also establishes some very important principles. "If a man seduces a virgin who is not pledged to be married and sleeps with her, he must pay the bride-price, and she shall be his wife" (Ex. 22:16). The formality of marriage is very important to God, as reflected in the laws of Moses.

Deuteronomy 22 refers to any woman who has sex before marriage as a prostitute. In 1 Cor. 6:15–16, 18, Paul instructs us: "Do you not know that your bodies are members of Christ Himself? Shall I then take the members of Christ and unite them with a prostitute? Never! Do you not know that he who unites himself with a prostitute is one with her in body? For it is said, 'The two will become one flesh.' . . . Flee from sexual immorality."

There's something you can learn from Deanna's dilemma. When doubts come, dig into the Scriptures for your answers instead of letting human reasoning take over. God's Word is the guide you need.

MEMORIZE

"There is a way that seems right to a man, but in the end it leads to death" (Prov. 14:12).

PICTURE THIS

PERSONALIZE AND READ OUT LOUD

What seems okay to me could be very dangerous to me spiritually. I need to check out everything with the Word of God.

PRAY THE VERSE, APPLYING IT TO YOUR LIFE

Dear God, keep me from thinking I'm so smart and that my ideas are the greatest. Help me to realize that anything that isn't in line with your Word could cause me great harm.

PLAN WITH GOD

Put your philosophy of life down on paper. Make it detailed and include the plans and goals you have for your life. (Be honest. Don't write something to make yourself look good.) Then ask your pastor or trusted Christian friend to examine your ideas in the light of God's Word. Ask for specific verses to correct your wrong ideas.

CHAPTER 30

Send the Devil's Packages Back Without Opening Them

Brent had only been a Christian two weeks, and he was really excited about his new life in Jesus. When he found out that a group of young people planned to go beach witnessing on Saturday, he found a replacement at work so he could go along. After a short orientation, he teamed up with Keith, who had been a Christian for a long time.

At the beach, they approached a couple guys. Keith smoothly opened a casual conversation, leading it around to spiritual things. He then asked Brent to give his testimony. Brent explained how Jesus had given him power to quit taking drugs, to stop skipping school, and to break off an immoral relationship with his girlfriend. The guys listened intently, and then Keith went on to explain the gospel. One of the guys decided to give his life to Jesus, and promised to come to Bible study on Tuesday night.

Brent felt elated. And as he and Keith walked along, he thought how neat it was to be part of God's team, doing work that would last for all eternity!

But at that very moment he saw a very shapely lady in a bikini. A flood of lustful thoughts rushed into his mind. Immediately, he was attacked by accusations: "See, you're no different than before. You'll never last as a Christian. The terrible thoughts you just had prove that you're unacceptable to God."

Keith noticed his silence and the pained expression on his face. "What's the matter?"

"I think I'm too sinful to keep witnessing," Brent replied. "I'd better just go home."

"What gave you that idea?" Keith asked in surprise.

"Did you see that blonde in the green bikini? Well, the thoughts I had after passing her were definitely x-rated."

"Brent," Keith explained, "I saw her, too. And the Devil dropped a pretty terrible idea into my head. But I've learned not to accept the thoughts he gives me. I turned my head immediately and started looking at the sailboats. I also said under my breath, "Devil I reject your thought. I'm going to keep my mind on Jesus. This is possible because I can do everything through him who gives me the strength" (Phil. 4:13).

"You see, Christians are still tempted. And temptation is *not* sin. Even Jesus was tempted. The Devil suggested that he jump off the highest point of the temple and commit suicide. Jesus didn't give the idea a second thought. He quoted Scripture to the Devil. So the thought the Devil gives you isn't sin—if you kick it out right away."

"I'm sure glad you clued me in," Brent thanked. "I had the impression I'd never get any lustful thoughts again. But now I know that when I get mail from the Devil, I can send back the packages unopened."

Luther tells this story. When a young man asked how to rid himself of evil thoughts, an old man gave him this advice. "Dear brother, you cannot prevent the birds from flying over your head, but you can certainly keep them from building a nest in your hair."*

---

*American Edition A.E. "Devotional Writings," *Luther's Works*, vol. 42, ed. by Martin O. Dietrich; gen. ed. Helmut Lehman, trans. Martin H. Bertram (Philadelphia: Fortress Press, 1969).

MEMORIZE

"Because he himself suffered when he was tempted, he is able to help those who are being tempted" (Heb. 2:18).

PICTURE THIS

PERSONALIZE AND READ OUT LOUD

Since Jesus was tempted, I also can expect to encounter temptation. Because Jesus suffered through temptations, He knows how I feel when trials hit me. He was always victorious, and He can help me.

PRAY THE VERSE, APPLYING IT TO YOUR LIFE

Dear God, thanks for sending Jesus to earth to suffer temptation. Thank you for understanding my problem with _____ . Thank you for helping me to meditate on Scripture.

PROJECT ENCOURAGEMENT

Copy Heb. 2:18 on a card. Keep a record of the number of times you're able to read it over and think about it this week. And trust Jesus to help you with your next temptation.

CHAPTER 31

How Is Temptation Like a Vacuum Cleaner Salesman?

Ashley often wished that her parents weren't so strict. Living under the same "eighteenth-century regulations" her parents had laid down for her brothers and sisters (who were much older than she) seemed too confining.

One of these rules was that she couldn't date until she was sixteen. Although she knew that God had commanded her to honor her father and mother, resentment boiled inside.

Chad was a tall blond who had recently moved to Indianapolis from North Dakota. He sat next to her in the trumpet section. He was friendly, studious, and athletic— plus he was a senior and he drove a sports car! She'd had a crush on him since September.

Then Chad invited her out for dinner. Even though her conscience begged with her to explain that she couldn't date him until August when she'd turn sixteen, she said she'd love to go.

She carefully planned her strategy: She would stay overnight with Kim, so her parents wouldn't find out about the date. Then she realized that Kim's folks might guess what she was up to, so she'd really have to ask Chad to pick her up at *Kathy's* house. Something whispered, *You're not going to get out of this one without telling a few lies.* But she reasoned that if her parents weren't so old-fashioned she wouldn't be forced to go to such extremes.

There were a lot of details to be worked out. She had

to bring her clothes for Friday's date to school piece by piece and send them home with Kathy. That way she could leave the house at 4:30, wearing blue jeans and carrying a small overnight case, which would arouse no suspicion. She asked Kim to keep the phone off the hook, so her mother couldn't possibly call. Carefully, she concocted an alibi to tell Chad. Another little voice informed her that this was her last chance to escape with her honesty intact—but she refused to listen.

At 6:00 P.M. on Friday, Ashley looked her best. One last five-second warning advised her to back out. But she'd gone too far to even think of it. Then Chad knocked at the door of Kathy's house, and they were off to Jim's Steak House where the two-for-the-price-of-one T-bone offer had people lined up out to the sidewalk. After an hour of pleasant conversation and joking, they were seated at a nice candlelit table—right next to Ashley's parents!

Maybe you don't like stories that have a "you-may-be-sure-that-your-sin-will-find-you-out" kind of plot. But these words are from the Bible, and in real life the narrative *always* ends like that. And if you want to avoid producing your own autobiography with similar episodes, you must learn the truth of 1 Cor. 10:13: "But when you are tempted, he [God] will also provide a way out so that you can stand up under it."

Larry Christenson has observed that most spiritual battles are won or lost at the threshold of the mind. That's because the easiest time to say no to temptation is *before* you've had any time to mull things over and rationalize your way into wrongdoing.

A fairly comfortable escape route was offered to Ashley when Chad first asked her out. Explaining the truth to him would have been relatively simple. The thought that she could make arrangements to stay overnight with Kim and have Chad pick her up at Kathy's offered another exit—a little harder to enter, but not that difficult. An alarm went off before she lied to Chad. Getting out of the situation, by then, required more humility and a loss of face, but it wasn't impossible. However, by the time Chad knocked on the door, the temptation to sneak out without her parents' permission was almost totally irresistible.

Anabel Gilham sums it up this way: "All sin is made up of component parts."

And temptation is like a vacuum cleaner salesman—the sooner you say no, the better. It's a lot easier to meet temptation at the door and say no than to kick it out once it's gotten inside your mind.

MEMORIZE

"No temptation has seized you except what is common to man. And God is faithful; he will not let you be tempted beyond what you can bear. But when you are tempted, he will also provide a way out so that you can stand up under it" (1 Cor. 10:13).

PICTURE THIS

PERSONALIZE AND READ OUT LOUD

I don't face any temptations that other people don't have. God promises that I'll never face any temptation too hard for me to overcome. And when I meet temptation, he'll show me the escape route so I can be victorious.

PRAY THE VERSE, APPLYING IT TO YOUR LIFE

Dear God, thank you that _____ (present temptation) is nothing so unusual. Thank you for your faithfulness. Thank you that, with you living through me, I can stand the pressure. Show me the exit you've prepared for me.

MAP OUT ESCAPE ROUTES

What are your three most frequent temptations? List the exit signs you usually pass before committing sin. (e.g., (a) I could kick out the bad thoughts I have about my brother, but instead I entertain them; (b) I could give my rights to Jesus, but instead I insist on them; (c) I could control my tongue, but instead I insult my brother.)

CHAPTER 32

Neon Lights, Fireworks, and Visions of Angels

Chris listened solemnly as his father passed sentence: "Give me the car keys and I'll keep them for a whole month. That will teach you never to lie to me about where you are going. Your mother and I have the responsibility to keep track of you and help you stay out of trouble."

Those last words touched off a seething resentment within Chris. He saw flashing red lights against the orange and yellow swirls on the den's wallpaper. The words read, "Honor your father and your mother." But Christopher decided that those orders were for little kids—and so he spouted off to his dad.

"I'm old enough to look out for myself. I'm the only guy in the junior class who has to face the 'Family Bureau of Investigation' every time I leave the house. I may just run away from home!"

In an instant, he was transferred to the locker room at school. Comments were getting more and more off-color. He remembered a dirty joke that was really very funny. This time he saw the neon lights silhouetted against the row of gray lockers. Their message flashed: "Nor should there be obscenity, foolish talk or coarse joking, which are out of place, but rather thanksgiving" (Eph. 5:4). But he really didn't want the guys to think he was from Nerdsville, so he told the joke and enjoyed being the center of attention for two whole minutes.

Next, he found himself in a social studies class. "How many of you really believe that God wrote the Bible?"

sneered the teacher. Now the neon lights lit up the black-board with these words: "If we endure, we will also reign with him. If we disown him, he will also disown us" (2 Tim. 2:12). But no one else raised a hand, so he gave silent assent as the teacher declared, "See, nobody believes such nonsense any more."

———————

At that moment, Chris woke up. His clock told him that it was 9:00 A.M., and the blaring TV in the next room assured him that his little brother was watching Saturday cartoons. He puzzled over his strange dream, and half-expected to see neon lights in the bathroom mirror when he got up.

The next morning, Sunday, was just like all the others he'd known—no nightmare to contemplate, a family breakfast of bacon and eggs and the usual rush to accomplish the sometimes difficult feat of getting four children and two parents properly outfitted, with Bibles tucked under their arms and all aboard for the fifteen-minute drive to church.

The pastor announced that his sermon topic was, "The Five Seconds That Decide the Difference Between Victory and Defeat." Christopher made up his mind to listen.

The pastor pointed out that the ancient Israelites could have been winners. "There were no temptations that could have overcome the children of God had they used the Word of God which they had *at the time.** It's the five seconds in which you decide whether or not to obey the Word of God that you *already know* that spells victory or defeat."

The pastor continued, "I don't counsel many people who have gotten into trouble because they were ignorant of the difference between right and wrong. Falling into sin is a result of deciding to do your own thing instead of obeying the principles found in the Bible."

Chris reflected back on his dream. He realized that real

———————

*Hugh Smith, *Overcoming Temptation,* p. 4.

life wasn't any different—except for the neon lights. He always had the same choice: obeying God's Word (whether or not he felt like it, even when the price of obedience was high, and in spite of the fact that he really thought he had a better idea), or falling into temptation. Chris began praying, "Lord, I want following your Word to become so automatic to me that it won't even take me five seconds to decide to obey you. The neon lights were nice, but having your Word hidden in my heart will work even better." He stopped his prayer in time to hear the pastor say, to his astonishment, "And you really don't need neon lights, fireworks, or voices of angels to stop you from sinning. God's Word alone will do the job—if you decide to obey it."

MEMORIZE

"Blessed are they who keep his statutes and seek him with all their heart. They do nothing wrong; they walk in his ways" (Ps. 119:2–3).

PICTURE THIS

PERSONALIZE AND READ OUT LOUD

God will bless me if I keep all His commands and go after Him with my whole heart. Then He will keep me from doing anything wrong and from straying from His path.

PRAY THE VERSE, APPLYING IT TO YOUR LIFE

Dear God, help me to follow all the rules you've put in the Bible. I want you more than anything else in the world. You've said that if I do, these two things will keep me from doing anything wrong. It seems too simple, Lord, but I believe you.

GET THE FACTS STRAIGHT

Make a list of temptations you keep falling for. With a concordance, or with the help of a friend who knows the Bible well, find scriptures that will enable you to obey your way to freedom. Meditate on these verses often.

CHAPTER 33

Don't Forget to Take Your Power Pills

Rick was browsing in a bookstore, waiting for his mother to finish all her shopping. A thick, black paperback caught his eye: *The Truth About Witchcraft: Scientific and Case Histories Prove Its Validity.* Curious, Rick picked up the book and started to leaf through it. He remembered his pastor's words, "The occult is nothing to play around with. Stay as far away from it as possible."

But, an inner voice reasoned, *a Christian should know what he's up against. Besides, this is a scientific study, not a book on black magic.* Then a headline caught his eye, "Witch doctor in Africa kills 1000 people with Voodoo." "Modern Massachusetts Witch Tried for Murder" looked just as intriguing.

Before he knew it, Rick had shelled out $5.95 and had stuffed his new purchase into the bag with the jacket he'd bought. By the time his mother appeared, her arms full of bundles, Rick was innocently scanning through the most recent issue of "Sports Illustrated."

Because it was summer and he only had a part-time job, Rick had a lot of time on his hands. The book on witchcraft was so interesting and so captivating that he read it from cover to cover and even bought the sequel.

One night he had a dream—about witches and demons, in which he was the victim—his own personal horror movie. In fact, he woke up trembling. He remembered the teaching he had received: "You have authority over the Devil. You tell him to leave in the name of Jesus and he must run."

Rick said it out loud. "Devil, I'm a King's kid. You can't touch me. Get out of here." But nothing happened.

Night after night the terrible dreams continued. Finally, he went to see his pastor.

"I just can't understand it," Rick began. "I've been having satanic nightmares. I have all my notes from the seminar on how to defeat the Devil. But when I rebuke Satan, it doesn't even help."

"Rick, may I ask you a question?" the pastor pressed. "Have you done anything to open the door for these demonic dreams?"

Finally, Rick confessed that he was still reading the occult books.

His pastor then shared with him a very important truth. "Every bit of authority that you have over the Devil comes from Jesus, and it depends on you being under the Lordship of Christ. The military policeman who disobeys his superiors and ends up in prison no longer has the right to give orders. In the same way, your disobedience to Jesus short-circuits your power system. You can't read occult books and then turn around and claim authority over demonic interference in your life. It's like locking the front door to keep the Devil out, while leaving the back door wide open! Repent of this sin," the Pastor urged. "Tear up your occult books and burn them. *Then* you can take authority over the Devil. In the name of Jesus and by the power of His blood you can really kick the Devil and his demons out of your room."

Remember that you'll be unable to exercise Jesus' power if you put up questionable pictures on your bulletin board, or bring in dirty magazines, or buy books that Jesus wouldn't approve of. On the plus side, each act of obedience to Jesus is like taking a power pill. Every time you obey, it enables you to exercise the authority Christ won for you when He died on the cross and rose again!

MEMORIZE

"Jesus replied, 'If anyone loves me, he will obey my teaching. My Father will love him, and we will come to him and make our home with him' " (John 14:23).

PICTURE THIS

PERSONALIZE AND READ OUT LOUD

If I love Jesus I'll obey Him even in _____ (something difficult for you to do). By my obedience I make room for Jesus to live inside me and experience His power through me.

PRAY THE VERSE, APPLYING IT TO YOUR LIFE

Dear God, I do love you so I'll obey you. I don't understand it all, but I know my obedience makes it possible for you and Jesus to live in me and through me. That's the kind of life I want.

OPERATION OBEDIENCE

1. Make a list of all the advantages of obeying God. (Jer. 7:23; Ex. 15:26; Deut 28:1–14; Josh. 1:7 might help.)
2. Write down areas in which you find it difficult to obey. Affirm your decision to follow God. If you can, place an appropriate Bible verse after each one. (e.g., I will not talk back to my mother. "Honor your father and your mother" [Exodus 20:12].)

CHAPTER 34

Imitate the Inventor of I-Have-Overcome-The-World Faith

Libby popped a load of clothes into the dryer and closed the glass door. Listless and discouraged, she stood staring at the turmoil going on inside. Swirls of color flipped and turned. Somehow she felt just like her red blouse—helpless in the mix, agitated to and fro by forces beyond her control, a prisoner with no chance of escape.

Problems, trials, temptations, spiritual growing pains, opportunities for exercising more faith—whatever term you preferred, she had them all. With her older brother on drugs and her parents continually arguing, her home was anything but a refuge. Libby's school was in a tough neighborhood, and kids like herself who tried to do what was right faced harassment from gangs and ridicule from classmates. Because her church seemed to be splitting, one could feel the tension even during services. Besides all this, she'd had a disagreement with her best friend, Meagan.

That was why Libby felt like the red blouse in the clothes dryer—but she had no assurance that it would all be over at the end of a half-hour cycle.

Tearfully, she agonized. "If only there were some way out."

Absent-mindedly, Libby went into her room and sat down on the bed. On her dresser, she saw the Bible verse poster that one of her Sunday school children had made for her. It read: "Let us fix our eyes on Jesus, the author and perfecter of our faith, who for the joy set before him endured the cross, scorning its shame, and sat down at the right hand of the throne of God. Consider him who endured such opposition from sinful men, so that you will not grow weary and lose heart" (Heb. 12:2–3).

She thought about Jesus. His life was no picnic. Even His own brothers refused to believe in Him. Peter was a smart-aleck, James and John were hotheads, and Judas was a thief as well as a traitor—not to mention the Pharisees, Sadducees, and lawyers He had to deal with. But His secret was that He never lost faith in the Father and His plans. He knew that God had everything under control and believed that the future God had designed for Him was worth it all.

Jesus holds the patent on the kind of faith that enables each one of us who is encased in a human body to live victoriously among hypocrites, heretics, half-hearted Christians, hatred, and heartbreak. His faith is worth imitating. His life merits consideration. *He* is the perfecter of our faith.

Libby realized that she was concentrating on her problems instead of focusing on Jesus and hanging on to her faith in His Word.

A passage she found in 1 Timothy clarified her course of action: "You may fight the good fight, holding on to faith and a good conscience. Some have rejected these and so have shipwrecked their faith" (1 Tim. 1:18–19). She knew that the only person who perfectly fought that good fight of faith was Jesus.

She *would* follow His example and triumph in the end! She'd stop listening to the Devil's lying voice ("Look, the people in your church don't practice what they preach, and neither do your parents. Things are utterly hopeless. You might as well give up"). She *would* stick with Jesus. Others could shipwreck their faith, but she didn't have to join them.

Jesus would show her how to be victorious in her home situation. Jesus would go to school with her every day. She would look at Jesus—not at those who didn't practice what they preached. With her eyes on Jesus she could apologize to Meagan. She determined to imitate the inventor of *I-have-overcome-the-world* faith.

MEMORIZE

"Consider him [Jesus] who endured such opposition from sinful men, so that you will not grow weary and lose heart" (Heb. 12:3).

PICTURE THIS

PERSONALIZE AND READ OUT LOUD

I will think about Jesus and imitate the way He handled worldly pressures. If He had to face _____ (problem you're encountering), I think He would _____ (action you feel Jesus would take in your situation). Then I won't get tired of resisting evil and feel like giving up.

PRAY THE VERSE, APPLYING IT TO YOUR LIFE

Dear God, I will let Jesus be my only example, then it won't throw me when "spiritual giant" Christians fail. Show me how to hang in there the way Jesus did. Keep me from getting worn out and discouraged.

MEDITATE ON SCRIPTURE

Reread the verse from Hebrews at every opportunity and let it soak into your spirit. Spend time considering the life of Jesus, and determine to follow Him. Fall asleep repeating the verse to yourself.

CHAPTER 35

Do You Hide Explosives in the Closet of Your Heart?

Casey had to admit that sixth-hour social studies class had been interesting. After a heated formal debate about gay rights, their teacher—whose unusual dress and effeminate manner had already aroused student rumors—launched into a passionate lecture.

"Some people," he declared, "are *born* homosexuals. Because they're a minority, they've been denied the right to express themselves fully. Americans accept people with black skin, with slanted eyes and with handicaps, but homosexuals are still discriminated against in this democratic country! It is no sin to be what you *are*. A person cannot change something he was born with."

As Casey listened, an inner horror had gripped him. That man was talking from experience; he must be right. And Casey feared that he himself was one of those unfortunate guys who was "born gay."

Because he was an extremely talented artist and didn't care for sports, he had always been rejected by the jocks. Even others noticed that he was different and his sixth-grade classmates had called him "queer." Deep down inside he felt more attracted to some guys than he did to girls. He remembered hearing that sodomy was the worst of sins. A voice seemed to be telling him, *Casey, you might as well stop being a Christian. You're already condemned. It isn't fair, but you were born a homosexual and there's no hope for you. You'll never be fulfilled unless you follow a gay lifestyle.*

For months his mind was in turmoil.

Finally, Greg, his compassionate Sunday school teacher noticed his troubled face. After class one day, he said gently, "I can tell that something's been bothering you lately. I'd like to talk to you about it. Maybe I can help."

Reluctantly, Casey agreed. It took him a full twenty minutes to come to the point, but finally he blurted out, "I guess I was born gay." Greg didn't even look shocked. He simply said, "That's a lie that the Devil gives to a lot of guys. I've got a friend who was caught up in a homosexual lifestyle before he became a Christian. Because he has decided to believe what God says about him and obey Jesus, he has changed drastically. He's not the same guy he was five years ago."

A week later, Greg and his friend Al came by for Casey, and they had a good talk. Al explained a lot of things.

"First of all," Al stated, "God didn't create any homosexuals. The Bible's definition of homosexuality is this: 'Men also abandoned natural relations with women and were inflamed with lust for one another. Men committed indecent acts with other men and received in themselves the due penalty of their perversion' (Rom. 1:27). God's love plus the pure, healthy love of other Christian men can fill the void in your life that right now makes you long for a wrong relationship with some other guy.

"Although a homosexual *act* is sin, the *temptation* is not," Al emphasized. "People are tempted to do all kinds of other unnatural things, like destroy their bodies with drugs, abuse children, engage in daredevil exploits in order to show off, or commit suicide. I might be tempted to jump from the Empire State Building, but I don't have to do it—and I don't have to consider myself *suicidal* just because the Devil placed that thought in my head. You don't have to call yourself homosexual, because of the temptation, either!"

Casey met with Greg and Al every week. They had Bible studies and fun times together. Casey actually began to believe that his problem wasn't too big for God. His awful fear began to leave. But he hated to think of what might have happened if he had never confided in anyone.*

So many sins could have been avoided if people, like Casey, had shared their temptations and fears with a mature Christian. Ask God to give you someone in whom you can confide. It's better not to hide any explosives in the closet of your heart.

---

*If you have a problem similar to Casey's, you can write to Exodus International, P.O. Box 2121, San Rafael, CA 94912 to find a Christian counseling service near you.

MEMORIZE

"Carry each other's burdens, and in this way you will fulfill the law of Christ" (Gal. 6:2).

PICTURE THIS

PERSONALIZE AND READ OUT LOUD

I will be willing to help other Christians with their problems and, in turn, share my burdens with them. Christ didn't intend that I, or any other believer, should go it alone.

PRAY THE VERSE, APPLYING IT TO YOUR LIFE

Dear God, give me wisdom and patience to help _____ with his/her present problems. Show me a mature Christian with whom I can share my problem of _____ (strongest temptation). I want to fulfill your law of love.

CURE THAT LONE-RANGER SYNDROME

Pray every day for a week, asking God to give you a mature Christian friend (of your sex), with whom you can share your problems. Then ask that person if you can meet every two weeks, or every month to share and pray. This is one of the best ways to keep temptations from growing into sins.

Self-Examination

Part IV. Hold That Line

1. _____
   is the Devil's introduction to temptation.
2. Temptation is a sin.   T   F
3. The Devil can put terrible thoughts into your mind,
   but if you reject them at once you have not sinned.
                                                               T   F
4. How is temptation like a vacuum cleaner salesman?
   _____
   _____
   _____
5. You always have a choice: _____
   or falling into temptation.
6. You lose your authority over the Devil
   _____ a. if you are disobedient to Jesus, the source of
           your authority.
   _____ b. if you don't talk to him in a loud voice.
   _____ c. if you forgot to pray that morning.
   _____ d. if you didn't use exactly the right words.

7. Are there areas of disobedience in your life that are short-circuiting the power you should exercise over Satan?

   ____

   What are they? ______________________________

   What are you going to do about them? ______________________________

   ____

8. Instead of looking at the hypocrites and half-hearted Christians around you, what should you do? ______________________________

   ____

9. Do you have a problem you should share with a mature Christian? __________ What is it? ______________________________

   ____

10. What are the only two weapons the Devil has? __________

    ______________ and ______________

---

1. Doubt that what God's word says is true; **2.** F; **3.** T; **4.** It's a lot easier to meet it at the door and say "no" than to kick it out of your mind; **5.** Obeying the Word of God you have at the moment; **6.** a; **7.** Personal; **8.** Admire and imitate Jesus; **9.** Personal; **10.** Deception and Manipulation.

Part Five

Push 'Em Back, Push 'Em Back, Way Back

CHAPTER 36

The Temptation That Didn't Make It to First Base

Jessica hurriedly wiped off the tables and counters in the restaurant where she worked. She said goodnight to Bob, owner of *Bob's Cafe* and longtime family friend. She ran to her mother's car and zipped over to the bank's drive-in teller to deposit $25 dollars in her savings account.

It was two minutes to nine. She had made it just before closing time.

The transaction completed, she put the car in gear and was about to drive off when she noticed something shiny on the ground. She got out of the car and picked up a small sequined purse. Opening it, she gasped with surprise as she counted the roll of bills. In her hand was $3,500!

Jessica's first thought was to bring the purse to the bank the next day, so that the lady who lost it could recover her money. Instantly, the Devil came up with a lot of other ideas—but to Jessica, anything other than strict honesty in money matters was unthinkable. She knew God saw her every action. She loved Him and wanted to please Him.

When she brought the money into the bank at 9:30 A.M., an older lady was there to greet her. She thrust a crisp hundred-dollar bill in her hands and exclaimed, "It's so nice to know that there are still some honest people left in the world!"

The reason that Jessica's temptation didn't even make

it to first base was that she really had no desire for money that wasn't rightfully hers.

Jesus never once fell for *any* temptation because His *only* desire was to obey God in every area of life. He put it this way: "The prince of this world [the Devil] is coming. He has no hold on me" (John 14:30). Jesus had no discontentment in His life. He harbored no bitterness. He had no inclination to trade righteousness for attention or apparent security. Satan just couldn't get in anywhere.

James 1:14 expresses it like this: "Each one is tempted when, by his own evil desire, he is dragged away and enticed." One very important way to prepare for your temptation test is to identify weak spots in your life and surrender your desires in this area to God.

If you, *un*like Jessica, love to spend money and just have to have the neatest clothes and the newest gadgets, you're leaving a door open to Satan. When opportunities arise to steal or shoplift, you could be convinced that having things is more important than honesty. If you resent your brilliant older brother, temptations to make fun of him or to get back at him will find fertile ground. If you want to get married more than you want to follow Jesus, you lay yourself wide open to falling into a lot of traps.

Check over your desires and decide to line them up with God's Word—regardless of your screaming emotions and mental excuses. When wayward wishes are brought under control, passing a temptation test is the easiest thing in the world.

MEMORIZE

"For I have come down from heaven not to do my own will but to do the will of him who sent me" (John 6:38).

PICTURE THIS

PERSONALIZE AND READ OUT LOUD

If Jesus came down from heaven only to do the will of the Father, who do I think I am doing my *own* will? If I decide that I am here to do God's will, not mine, I can shut the door on a lot of temptations.

PRAY THE VERSE, APPLYING IT TO YOUR LIFE

(**Warning: This prayer may be dangerous—unless of course, you really mean it.**) Dear God, right now I'm deciding that I'm here to do *your* will, not mine. I know _____ (something hard) is your will, and I'll do it with your help.

IDENTIFY YOUR DANGEROUS DESIRES

First, make a list of *everything* you'd like to have (e.g., a good-looking boyfriend/girlfriend, Calvin Klein jeans, an A in physics, a shorter nose, etc.). Then circle those wants that could easily get out of hand and become more important to you than doing God's will. Find scripture (or get help to do so) that you can memorize to help keep those desires in line. (e.g. shorter nose; "But who are you, O man, to talk back to God? Shall what is formed say to him who formed it, 'Why did you make me like this?' " [Rom. 9:20].)

CHAPTER 37

Don't Be Hoggish!—Unless What You Want Is More of Jesus

Danny attended a "Winter-tainment" weekend with his friend Paul—and what a blast he had! After a day of skiing, skating, and tobogganing, 300 teenagers packed into a gymnasium for an evening rally. There was some enthusiastic singing, followed by a dynamic speaker who challenged everyone to make a commitment to Christ.

Danny sensed a deep conviction in his heart and responded to the invitation. The speaker gave each of them a New Testament—and some words of advice. One thing especially stuck in Danny's mind: "Find yourself a good church, where there are Bible studies and where people believe and follow the Word of God."

Since Danny had never gone to church in his life, he didn't know where to start. He went to church with his friend Paul for a little while.

One Sunday evening, the pastor asked for "testimonies." A man got up and proclaimed, "I accepted Jesus as my Savior fifty years ago, and I've never been sorry." A younger lady shared, "I rededicated my life to Jesus on July 6, 1984, and I've been walking with the Lord ever since." After hearing a couple of others, Danny assumed that a "testimony" was declaring publicly something God had done for a person years ago.

When Nick invited Danny to his church, he discovered a different type of testimony. The pastor had asked, "What has Jesus done for you *this week*?" A fifteen-year-old girl explained, "I prayed for money to go on the youth retreat.

Yesterday, I received a fifty-dollar check in the mail from my aunt in California." A man stood to his feet: "You don't just dedicate your life to Jesus once—you do it over and over again. This week I was asked to do something dishonest at work. I chose to obey God and risk losing my job. I carefully explained to my boss why I couldn't fulfill his orders. At first he threatened to fire me, but then the president found out about it and gave me my boss's job!"

Danny noticed that these people lived as though they could never get enough of God. They didn't just dwell on something He had done in the past. They were much more interested in what God was going to do today. It was like they wanted to receive more and more of Jesus' life. Danny decided that he, too, wanted to live like that.

One of the most effective ways to defeat Satan in your life is to be constantly expecting and receiving more of the supernatural life of Jesus. At all cost, avoid the "saved, sanctified and *petrified*" syndrome! "Because of the Lord's great love we are not consumed, for his compassions never fail. They are new every morning" (Lam. 3:22–23). But if you don't depend on that new grace each day, you just might feel overwhelmed.

Possibly the best definition of a Christian is the one given by the apostle Paul: "Christ in you, the hope of glory" (Col. 1:27). And probably the best formula for victorious Christian living is that given by John the Baptist: "He must become greater; I must become less" (John 3:30).

If Jesus is really alive and growing in you, there's always something different to learn, newer ways to turn your life over to Him, greater security to experience and an increasing denial of self so that Christ's life can freely flow through you. This life of *go-for-it* faith is never boring. There will be growing pains and times when your mind cannot grasp what is going on. Even in defeats you can reach out for more of Jesus. Unpleasant operations will be necessary to remove some "cancer" of self that prevents the life of Jesus from increasing in you. But there will be great victories.

Becoming a Christian is a new birth, but *being* a Christian is letting that new life in Jesus grow in you, knowing that you are "predestined to be conformed to the likeness of his Son" (Rom. 8:29).

Don't try to "arrive" spiritually. That's an ego trip reserved for deceived people. Thank God for each special experience He has given you—but don't live in the past. Jesus has more of His life, more of His power, more of His love and more of His grace just for you. Don't be hoggish—unless what you want is more of Jesus!

MEMORIZE

"But one thing I do: Forgetting what is behind and straining toward what is ahead, I press on toward the goal to win the prize for which God has called me heavenward in Christ Jesus" (Phil. 3:13–14).

PICTURE THIS

PERSONALIZE AND READ OUT LOUD

I will make it a point *not* to live in the past, *not* even to rely on yesterday's mountaintop experiences with God. Instead, I go forward, expecting God to do even greater things in the future. I'll cooperate in every way I can to fulfill the goal God has for me and to win the prize—everything God has planned for me in heaven!

PRAY THE VERSE, APPLYING IT TO YOUR LIFE

Dear God, forgive me for being proud of _____ (some spiritual experience or accomplishment) and for not being willing to put _____ (past failure) behind me. Paul forgot about yesterday and kept running toward the goal. I better do the same. God, I promise to serve you today, tomorrow, and the next day. Thank you that the prize for fighting the good fight of faith is well worth the effort!

REINFORCE SOME RESOLUTIONS

1. List your top spiritual experiences: _____

   Thank God for each one of them, but resolve not to live in the past and to continually seek more of God.
2. List some dreams you have for the future: _____

PRAYER

Dear God, I determine to let you be God. I will not live for my goals but for the goal of obtaining more of the life of Jesus and getting to know Him better and better.

CHAPTER 38

Winning the War Against Feelings

Rosa pulled the covers up over her head, and her tired body sank into the soothing warmth of her water bed. It had been a hard week and she welcomed Friday night. Because she'd had to work overtime *and* study for three exams she was totally exhausted.

Pondering her plans for the next day, however, gave her a special sense of satisfaction: She'd sleep in, relax, take an afternoon nap, and allow a full three hours to get ready to go to the concert with Bill.

But at 7:00 A.M., Rosa heard her if-there's-such-a-thing-as-a-new-creature-in-Christ-you'd-better-prove-it-at-home mother yelling from the bottom of the stairway, "Rosa, it's time to get up! Remember, you promised you'd help me clean the kitchen. Well, today's the day."

Rosa's body and emotions rebelled. After such a tough week, she deserved a rest. Couldn't her mother show any consideration? She knew that Rosa had wanted to go out with Bill for a whole year and that tonight's date was very special. It just wasn't fair. Besides, when her mother cleaned the kitchen it took all day.

Rosa wanted so much to scream, "No, I won't! Let me sleep. You're not being reasonable. I promised to clean the kitchen, but not today." But she remembered her pastor's words: "If the Devil can entice you to live according to your feelings, instead of by the part of God's Word that applies to your situation, he'll win and you'll lose."

Rosa knew what God's Word to her was at that moment. She had just memorized Phil. 2:14: "Do everything without complaining or arguing." She knew she couldn't pamper her tired body instead of obeying Jesus. And she couldn't put Bill before God.

In order to lay down the law to her body and emotions, she said it out loud: "I will obey God's Word and forget about my feelings."

When her mother's second call came—complete with turned-up volume and angry words—Rosa answered like a champion who had just won, even though the competition was fierce: "I'm getting dressed, Mom, and I'll be right down."

Sensing Jesus' presence, Rosa put her heart into washing walls, scrubbing cupboards and scouring the stove. It took all day. When they finished, she was as proud of the kitchen as her mother.

Glancing at the clock, however, she panicked. It was 5:30! That gave her only one hour to try to look her best for her evening with Bill. A "Mother-now-I-won't-have-time-to-get-ready-for-my-date-and-it's-all-your-fault" almost escaped from her lips. Again, Rosa had to choose between feelings and God's Word. She took her stand on Scripture: "Do everything without complaining." Instead of grumbling and working herself into a tizzy, she prayed: "Oh Lord, help me to hurry and to look my best!"

And God answered her prayer. By 6:27, she was completely ready. When she answered the doorbell, Bill grinned at her. "You look great! I'll bet you spent all afternoon fixing your hair."

"As a matter of fact," Rosa replied, "I spent all day cleaning the kitchen. If you had come an hour ago, you'd have caught me in dirty blue jeans with greasy, stringy hair and no make-up."

"When I talked to you yesterday," Bill remembered, "you said that you planned to take it easy all day. What made you change your mind?"

When Rosa related the whole story, Bill confided, "I want to follow God completely. In fact, the reason I asked you out is because I wanted to get to know a girl with real character. It looks like I made a good choice."

Rosa smiled—and silently prayed, "Thank you, God. Thank you for helping me win the war against feelings."

MEMORIZE

"I have hidden your word in my heart that I might not sin against you" (Ps. 119:11).

PICTURE THIS

PERSONALIZE AND READ OUT LOUD

I will memorize and internalize God's Word. I will follow what God says, instead of being driven by my feelings.

PRAY THE VERSE, APPLYING IT TO YOUR LIFE

Dear God, thank you for your Word. Show me how to think, breathe and live your Word. Help me to avoid sin by constantly obeying your commandments.

INSTALL YOUR ANTI-SIN-LISTIC MISSILE SYSTEM

List the recurring sins in your life. Beside each one write a verse, which if obeyed would eliminate that wrong doing. (If you don't know your Bible well enough to find the verses, get someone to help you.) Determine to digest the verses spiritually and let them sink into your heart.

CHAPTER 39

"Grow Away" Those Problems That Just Won't Go Away!

When her father announced that the family would spend their vacation traveling to Denver and camping in the Rockies with the Smiths, Brooke nearly groaned out loud. She just couldn't share the enthusiasm of her little sister whose only goal was to see "a real live bear."

Brooke could only remember how awkward she had felt during the visit they'd made three years ago. The Smith's son Steve was exactly her age. Because the Smith's had once been next-door neighbors, Steve and Brooke had practically grown up together. When they were both eight, the Smiths had moved to Colorado.

Six years later, Steve bore no resemblance to the cute little boy who had protected her from dogs and climbed trees to get apples so her dolls could have real apple pie. At fourteen, he'd been a short, skinny loudmouth, an unbearable tease, and a practical joker who didn't know when to quit.

Now, just the thought of having to spend ten days within earshot of Steve inspired Brooke to buy ten new cassettes for her walkman so she could tune him out.

When they arrived at the Smith home, though, she saw a tall, handsome young man with a ready smile and a courteous manner. If it hadn't been for his red hair and freckles, she never would have guessed it was Steve. Her heart skipped a beat, and she decided that this just might be the best vacation she'd ever had!

That night before going to bed she read a chapter from

her Bible. A special verse caught her eye: "For you have been born again, not of perishable seed, but of imperishable, through the living and enduring word of God" (1 Pet. 1:23). She saw something new: That imperishable seed planted in each believer, if given the opportunity, will grow. As it grows it will replace garbage-like thoughts, weeds of sin—even mental blocks and personality defects. The very life of God is contained in that seed which is placed in the heart of each real Christian!

Just as growing up a little had resolved problems for her and Steve, spiritual growth could help her overcome some present trials and temptations. Brooke decided to do everything possible to give herself the right atmosphere to grow as a Christian. She knew she needed to put more and more of God's Word in her heart. If she didn't spend time talking to God and listening for His voice, she realized she'd never be more like Jesus.

Now, she also saw how some things she'd always considered as negatives could provide her with an atmosphere for spiritual growth. If she chose to listen to good Christian music, it would help her become a stronger Christian. If she read only material that would build her up, she could grow a lot faster. And she could choose recreation that would bring her closer to Jesus.

She knew that difficulties wouldn't just go away. She also realized if there was sin involved, she had to repent totally before there would be any progress. She also saw that it is possible to "grow away" from many of her problems and she resolved to do her part.

MEMORIZE

"But grow in the grace and knowledge of our Lord and Savior Jesus Christ. To him be glory both now and forever" (2 Pet. 3:18).

PICTURE THIS

PERSONALIZE AND READ OUT LOUD

I will grow spiritually if I put myself in a position to receive God's grace. Right now, I rid myself of bitterness about _____ so I can get special kindness and mercy from God to handle this situation. I will internalize more of God's living Word so I can get to know Jesus in a deeper way. I praise God for His grace!

PRAY THE VERSE, APPLYING IT TO YOUR LIFE

Dear God, thank you that as I experience more of your grace and learn to know you better, I will grow up into Christ and have even more to praise you for.

PIN IT DOWN

Copy 2 Pet. 3:18 on a card. Refer to it throughout the day and let its words become part of you. Go to sleep repeating, "To him be glory both now and forever."

CHAPTER 40

The Failure That Made Victory Possible

Gary felt even smaller and skinnier than he looked in the mirror—more insignificant and rejected, too.

Because his father was being transferred to Texas, this was Gary's last day at Roosevelt High. Nobody had organized a goodbye party for him, and only a few kids even bothered to wish him well. Dejectedly, he stuffed the few things he kept in his locker into a big shopping bag. Everyone always cleared out quickly on Fridays and the school was practically empty.

For some reason, Gary decided to take a final tour of the building where he'd spent three and one half years. Worried thoughts kept tormenting him: *If I haven't made any close friends here in all this time, what's it gonna be like in Texas?* Entering the gym, he saw a letter jacket on the bleachers. Absentmindedly, he picked it up. He noticed that it was his size and that all the medals were in track and skiing.

Suddenly, an ingenious idea occurred to him. There was plenty of room for the jacket in the bottom of his shopping bag. No one would notice if he walked out with it. If he took off all the track pins he wouldn't have to compete, and yet he could wear it in his new school, posing as a Minnesota ski hero! Maybe then he'd gain some respect.

And so "Gary the Great" registered at Booker T. Washington High School in Dallas, sporting a letter jacket with ski medals. On his first day, he managed to attract quite a bit of attention. But because Pam, who sat next to him in English class, also attended the church his parents had chosen, his lies followed him to Sunday school class.

One day, Pam's comments to his mother blew his cover completely. He was totally embarrassed and ashamed. Worst of all, he had made a fool of himself in front of Pam, the one person he most wanted to impress.

Fortunately for Gary, his Sunday school teacher, Tom, drove over to his house to see him the next day. "Gary," he said reassuringly, "all of us fail. But there is a way to turn failure into victory. The first thing you have to do is repent of your lying and resentment against God for not giving you an athlete's body. Admit you stole that letter jacket. Saying, 'I'm sorry I got caught' just won't do. You need to tell God, 'I'm guilty of lying and stealing and trying to be somebody I'm not. I hate these terrible sins against you and I'm going to change.' Then you can accept God's total forgiveness. It's also important to forgive yourself, instead of dwelling on the incident forever."

Tom went on, "It's your responsibility as well, to send the letter jacket back with an apology to the boy who owns it. And in order to come clear, you must also tell the truth to everyone you lied to, no matter how much you hate doing it. Be ready to accept all the shame and embarrassment and any other discipline God has for you. Remember, God only 'spanks' His kids because He loves them and wants the best for them. All the pain will be worth it in the end.

"You can learn something very important from this incident," Tom concluded, "and if you do, all your suffering won't be wasted. Not accepting yourself as God made you is very dangerous, because it opens the door for all kinds of sins. Since I went through the same thing as a teenager, I feel I can help you—and someday God will use you to help another person, too."

Gary got the message. When he asked God to forgive him, he didn't blame anything or anyone else. He realized how greatly he'd sinned against God by lying and stealing. He resolved never to do such a thing again. He also asked

God to forgive him for not accepting his short, skinny body, and he thanked God for making him the way he was—a perfect frame in which to "show off" the life of Jesus. He accepted God's forgiveness. When kids asked him, "Where's your letter jacket?" he told them the whole truth. A few made fun of him. But he decided that since he had brought it on himself, he wasn't going to sweat it.

With Tom's help, Gary started learning how to really receive God's love, to be thankful for everything and to get all his acceptance from God, rather than from those around him. After six months, he regarded the whole incident as the failure that made victory possible. As he relaxed and accepted himself just the way God made him, a whole lot of things began to change. Pam admired the way he handled failure so much that he got up enough courage to ask her out. And when he left for college in another state, his new friends did organize a goodbye party—just for him.

MEMORIZE

"But who are you, O man, to talk back to God? Shall what is formed say to him who formed it, 'Why did you make me like this?' " (Rom. 9:20).

PICTURE THIS

PERSONALIZE AND READ OUT LOUD

I, _____ , will not complain about the way God made me. After all, the Divine Potter formed me with both time and eternity in mind. I trust that He knows best and I thank Him.

PRAY THE VERSE, APPLYING IT TO YOUR LIFE

Forgive me for questioning the way you made me. Thank you that you have all power to change me and heal me. I will put everything into your hands and trust you.

BANISHING BITTERNESS

Make a list of the physical characteristics you've always wished you had the ability to change. Repent of resentment you've had against God for these things. Remind yourself that God's purposes are eternal—not tied to the world's present idea of "good-looking." Also remember that God is all-powerful, able to change and to heal. Relax and let Him be God.

CHAPTER 41

You're Not Here to Lead a Treasure Hunt

Rachael tried desperately to brush away invading thoughts.

Frantically, she attempted to do something with droopy hair that defied extra-body shampoo and had responded very poorly to a perm. Besides her complex about having "mouse hair," she thought she was too tall, too thin, and that her feet were much too large to be considered feminine.

Deciding that standing in front of the full-length mirror was making her depressed, she started looking through her closet. Surveying her clothes, however, failed to cheer her up. She couldn't find anything sharp to wear to the evangelistic picnic her Sunday school class had planned. This was the day they were going to put into practice what they had learned about personal evangelism, and she thought looking good might overcome some of her nervousness.

Rachael wondered if she really could find a time during the day to witness to one of the new girls they had invited. She worried about how she would come across. Everyone labeled her a "brain" and she battled a shyness that made her feel socially awkward. She wished she could be pretty, vivacious, and "Miss Personality Plus." Then others would certainly be willing to listen when she shared Jesus with them.

When Mary, her Sunday school teacher, picked her up early to help make sandwiches, she noticed that Rachael looked discouraged. "You look down. What's the problem?" Mary asked. And Rachael shared her feelings.

"Rachael," Mary encouraged, "There's a verse in the Bible that you need to understand: 'But we have this treasure in jars of clay to show that this all-surpassing power is from God and not from us' (2 Cor. 4:7). We're the jars of clay and Jesus is the treasure. God planned it that way so it would be obvious that the glory belongs to Jesus, not to us. The person who led me to Christ really wasn't very cool, but I could see that Christ had really made a difference in her life. I thought that if Christ could help her— and she had many more problems than I did—He certainly could help me. Just remember that you're exactly the right container to display the wonderful treasure Jesus really is."

Rachael remembered that when they reached the picnic. She made friends with Tammy and started to tell her what a wonderful friend Jesus is. Then Tammy confided, "You're the first timid person I've ever met who claimed to be a Christian. I thought that only self-confident kids who don't mind standing out from the crowd could follow Jesus. If Jesus helps you overcome shyness, I'm interested."

Under her breath, Rachael prayed, "Thank you God for making me the way I am. Thank you for putting the treasure of yourself in a clay jar just like me."

Although it's right to "look your best for Jesus" and to be conscious of making a good impression on non-Christians, it's wrong to forget that you're a clay jar. If you try to be "Super Man Christian" or "Wonder Woman Witness," attempting to eliminate your humanness, you'll fall into temptation. Either you'll become discouraged because you didn't live up to *your* goal, or you'll begin faking it—pretending to be someone you're not.

Never excuse anything that is contrary to God's Word—not even "shyness." But remember that the containers God chose to demonstrate His power had weaknesses. Gideon had an inferiority complex. Moses most likely stuttered. Jeremiah was sometimes depressed. Peter made rash decisions. Thomas doubted. The list goes on. God's plan hasn't changed. He still puts the priceless treasure of himself into people who talk too much, who lack poise, who have trouble with math, and who bite their fingernails. Accept the fact that you, too, are human.

If you concentrate on Jesus, totally, forgetting about your idiosyncrasies and personality problems, others will see so much treasure that the vase it comes in will make no difference. You're not to lead a treasure hunt—Jesus should become the only thing that people notice about you.

MEMORIZE

"When they saw the courage of Peter and John and realized that they were unschooled, ordinary men, they were astonished and they took note that these men had been with Jesus" (Acts 4:13).

PICTURE THIS

PERSONALIZE AND READ OUT LOUD

When people see what Jesus has placed in me and they realize that I'm _____ , _____ , and _____ (inadequacies and weaknesses), they'll be surprised. Then they'll be able to see that I was able to accomplish what I did because of spending so much time with Him.

PRAY THE VERSE, APPLYING IT TO YOUR LIFE

Dear God, put _____ and _____ (qualities you need to serve God) in me. I don't care if I don't have _____ (qualities you've always admired). I just want people to notice Jesus in me.

BUILDING CHRIST-CONFIDENCE

Write this verse on a card and refer to it throughout the day, reminding yourself that people can tell the difference if you spend time with Jesus. As you close your eyes tonight, reflect on the verse.

CHAPTER 42

Are You Suffocating In Your Isolation Booth?

Mark wished he were back in California.

Adjusting to living in a small midwest town was more than he bargained for. The kids at school treated the "new boy from California" like some kind of transplant from Mars, and they thought he dressed a little weird. If he didn't feel like going bowling or playing miniature golf, there was *nothing* to do. And the problem would get worse in the winter when he'd either have to learn to ice skate or become a social outcast.

But the hardest part was that the church here was nothing like the one he'd left behind. He thought the pastor's sermons were boring. Only five kids showed up at the youth Bible study. They didn't know how to really dig into the Word, and it was obvious that they knew nothing about the deeper Christian life. Mark decided that he was too spiritual for the group and that he'd get more out of doing his own Bible studies at home.

In a letter to Pastor Jim, he explained the whole situation and his decision to hold a private Bible study. Soon he discovered a super TV program on Saturday nights and found out that sleeping in on Sunday morning felt good. His plan for attacking the book of Ezekiel got as far as chapter three.

When Mark got Pastor Jim's reply to his letter, he opened the envelope eagerly. He began reading:

Dear Mark,
Thanks for your letter. I'm sure that it's difficult to

adjust to new surroundings. But you must remember that nothing changes God's clear, biblical directions. "Let us not give up meeting together, as some are in the habit of doing, but let us encourage one another—and all the more as you see the Day approaching" (Heb. 10:25). "Make every effort to keep the unity of the Spirit through the bond of peace" (Eph. 4:3). "So that there should be no division in the body [of Christ], but that its parts should have equal concern for each other" (1 Cor. 12:25). You can't fully obey any of these scriptures if you're not part of some local church.

You need to be aware of the fact that it's Satan's strategy to isolate Christians. If he can get you to think you're too good for the Christians around you, he can use your pride to try to make you think you've got a deeper knowledge of the Bible than anyone else. This will lead you off track. If he can convince you that these Christians don't really accept you, he can turn you into a bitter, lonely person. The Devil is also good at giving people lazy habits, like sleeping in on Sunday morning and watching TV instead of going to prayer meeting. The truth is that you need other Christians and they need you. Just as it's simple to break one pencil alone and impossible to break twenty at once, it's easier for the Devil to deceive a loner than a whole group of Christians.

Besides, each Christian group and each church has strengths and weaknesses. Maybe you can teach this youth group more about how to study the Bible. But also be open to be taught by them in other areas.

May God bless you!

Pastor Jim

Mark decided to go to the youth group on Saturday night. The pastor explained that a young couple had just moved into town and that the husband had injured his back so he couldn't work. Their home needed to be fixed up and they hardly had food to eat.

Leslie suggested that they take up an offering and buy groceries for them. It was Craig's idea that the whole group spend the next three Saturdays fixing and painting all the rooms. "After that, we can share the gospel with them," Holly offered.

Mark had never seen such generosity and love. He certainly did have something to learn from these Christians.

At 10:00 P.M. on the third Saturday, they finished their project. The grateful couple was ready to hear the gospel message they presented, and both of them accepted Christ. At this point Mark was thinking, *And I could have missed all this just to watch some silly TV show.*

He realized how close he had come to suffocating in his isolation booth.

MEMORIZE

"Let us not give up meeting together, as some are in the habit of doing, but let us encourage one another—and all the more as you see the Day approaching" (Heb. 10:25).

PICTURE THIS

PERSONALIZE AND READ OUT LOUD

I will not manufacture excuses for staying home from church. I'll attend and go with the idea of encouraging someone else. I know that we all need to help each other, because Jesus is coming soon.

PRAY THE VERSE, APPLYING IT TO YOUR LIFE

Dear God, help me to be faithful in meeting with others for worship, prayer, and Bible study. Make me an encouragement to other Christians. Jesus, thank you that you're coming back again soon.

ELIMINATING THAT EXCUSE HANDBOOK

List all the excuses you've used to skip church or Bible study. Cross out each one and write out Heb. 10:25 over it.

CHAPTER 43

Wearing the Right Wardrobe—And Winning

There was an air of excitement as Edison High kicked off to Central. This was the championship game!

Bryon, the quarterback for Central, couldn't wait to get his hands on that ball. A third-down fumble put the pigskin in their possession. As he called out the signals, he happened to look down and realized that he was playing barefoot in his pajamas! Sudden fear gripped him as helmeted monsters with cleats for claws rushed toward him after he got the ball.

He was sacked for a fifteen-yard loss and badly beaten up.

As he took the next snap from center, such panic seized him that he started running from would-be tacklers—only to be brought down bruised and bloody. Fighting dizziness and trying to rise to his feet, he heard the fans booing. . . .

Just then Bryon's alarm clock went off. He awakened from his nightmare, thankful that the game was on Friday and he could play it in full uniform.

Although most of us would never want to be on a football field in pajamas, we often face the battle of life—with its temptations and trials—just as unprepared. Because the Bible clearly tells us what to wear, it's our fault if we venture forth without our proper uniform and then experience defeat. If, however, you decide each day to don the armor outlined for us in Ephesians 6, you'll stack up more and more points in your victory column.

First, we're told, "Stand firm then, with the belt of truth buckled around your waist" (Eph. 6:14). For the Roman soldier, the belt was an apron made of thick leather, which covered vital organs and supported his sword. It was the most basic part of his armor. Because total truth will nip temptation in the bud, it is also the first thing you must put on in order to stand against Satan. Believe what God's Word says about you, your friends, and the world. Determine to live the truth without exaggeration, rationalization, giving false impressions, or cheating just a little. Truth demolishes Satan's strongest weapon—the lie.

The Scriptures also instruct us to have the breastplate of righteousness in place. Charles Stanley, in his book *Temptation*, says, "The breastplate of righteousness is to guard us from making decisions based on what we *feel* rather than on what we *know* to be right." "The end justifies the means" is one of the Devil's oldest cliches. Satan just can't get you if you choose to do what is correct—regardless of how you feel, how much it will cost, or the consequences you'll have to face.

Your shoes must be "the readiness that comes from the gospel of peace" (v. 15), which is also translated, "the preparation of the gospel of peace." The root for the Greek word translated "readiness" or "preparation" means "to shimmer like gold or like the clear sky." To me, this signifies an experiential appreciation of the value of the Christian message, which gives us peace with God and with those around us. Peace is an extremely important weapon in spiritual warfare. The agitated, the angry, and the anxious lose their heads when Satan attacks. Those who know the power of the gospel, who allow it to bring peace within and who spread that peace around, will not easily be tripped by temptation.

Next, we are told, "Take up the shield of faith, with which you can extinguish all the flaming arrows of the evil one" (v. 16). Don't let the Devil steal your belief that God can do *anything*. Without that, every problem is monumental; but with faith all things are possible.

The helmet we wear is the "assurance of our salvation." God has saved us not only from hell, but from sin, too. We have the potential to say no to Satan's suggestions.

The Word of God is our sword. The Devil is afraid of the Word of God. It's the defensive weapon Jesus used against Satan and his demons. It will work for you.

Charles Stanley suggests that, every day even before you get out of bed, you consciously put on your spiritual armor to face the day's schedule. For example, say to yourself: "I'm going to wear truth and righteousness today, and I won't even think of cheating on the geometry test. I will value the peace God gives, so I won't get ruffled by the teasing and unkind remarks I hear in gym class. I'll take the shield of faith and believe that God will give me the strength not to talk back to my mother, even if she's in a bad mood. I'll put on the helmet of salvation and not listen to the Devil's doubts. And I'll use this part of God's Word, 'I can do everything through him who gives me strength' " (Phil. 4:13).

This is a *great* way to start the day! I've tried it. Why don't you?

MEMORIZE

"Therefore, put on the full armor of God, so that when the day of evil comes, you may be able to stand your ground" (Eph. 6:13).

PICTURE THIS

PERSONALIZE AND READ OUT LOUD (IF YOU INTEND TO DO IT!)

I will consciously put on all God's armor—truth, righteousness, the peace that the gospel gives, faith, understanding of my salvation, and God's Word in my heart—each day. Then, when disaster strikes I'll be able to stand my ground.

PRAY THE VERSE, APPLYING IT TO YOUR LIFE

Lord, help me to obey your command to put on your armor. Right now I need it for _____ . Keep me from falling in this evil world.

PREPARE TO FOLLOW GOD'S INSTRUCTION

Make a poster for your room reminding you to put on God's armor every day. Maybe you can draw a soldier, or do a series of cartoons. If not, creatively arrange the words, truth, righteousness, faith, etc., on your poster.

Self-Examination

Part V. Push 'Em Back, Push 'Em Back, Way Back

1. It's easy to pass temptation tests
   _____ a. if you've memorized the whole Bible.
   _____ b. if you're a straight A student.
   _____ c. if you've never been into "serious sin," like drugs and stealing and illicit sex.
   _____ d. if you've surrendered *all* your desires to Jesus.

2. Some safeguards against temptation are:
   _____ a. arriving spiritually.
   _____ b. constantly expecting and receiving more of the supernatural life of Jesus.
   _____ c. letting "He must become greater; I must become less" function in your life.
   _____ d. exercising "go-for-it" faith.

3. You win against temptation when
   _____ a. you obey God's Word, even though it's hard.
   _____ b. you follow your feelings.
   _____ c. you go along with the crowd.
   _____ d. you do what comes naturally.

4. The Bible teaches that you're born again of imperishable seed. What can you do to help that seed grow?

_____

_____

5. Which is *not* a step in handling failure?
   _____ a. Confess and forsake your sin.
   _____ b. Go around for a long time feeling sad and doing penance.
   _____ c. Apologizing and making up for your wrongdoing.
   _____ e. Accepting God's discipline and forgiving yourself.

6. But we have this treasure in_____ (2 Cor. 5:7).

7. I need to be part of a local church, because _____

_____

_____

8. List the armor you need to put on each day: _____

_____

_____

9. Who must be the *only* source of your significance and self-worth? _____

10. When the Devil puts a bad thought into your mind, what should you do? _____

_____

1. d; 2. b, c, d; 3. a; 4. Put God's Word in your heart, listen to His voice, provide yourself with an atmosphere of Christian growth—godly music, edifying reading material, wholesome recreation, etc.; 5. b; 6. Jars of clay; 7. It's a biblical command, it's Satan's strategy to isolate Christians so he can get them off-track, I need other Christians; 8. Belt of truth, breastplate of righteousness, shoes of readiness that come from the gospel of peace, shield of faith, helmet of salvation, sword of the Spirit; 9. God; 10. Kick it out immediately.

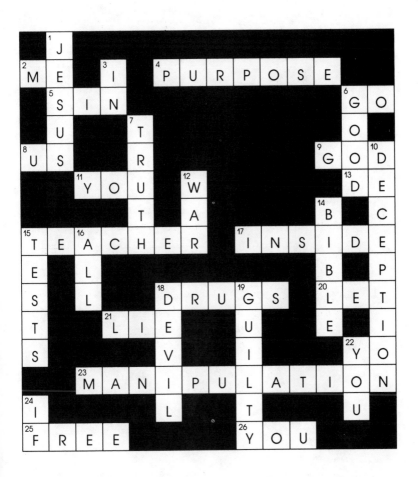